COMPENDIUM OF WISDOM, WEALTH AND POWER

David S. Philemon

Royal Diadem Publishing Inc.

Dedication

*To the Almighty God, my Rock, Refuge, and Source of all
wisdom and strength. Thank You for Your unwavering love,
grace, and the purpose You've placed within me. May this book
bring glory to Your name and draw others closer to You.*

*And to my beloved spiritual parents, Dr. Paul and Dr. Mrs. Becky
Paul Enenche, who have faithfully nurtured and guided me
in this journey. Your example of unwavering devotion, godly
counsel, and compassionate care has been a beacon of light
and strength in my life. Thank you for standing as pillars of
faith and for your steadfast commitment to the Kingdom.*

CONTENTS

Title Page

Copyright

Dedication

Acknowledgments

Chapter One   1

Strength For Destiny   2

Chapter Two   7

The Best Resides In You   8

Chapter Three   14

Navigating Spiritual Instructions & Embracing God's   15
Guidelines For Success

Chapter Four   22

Courageous Faith & Unlocking Your Path To Success And   23
Favor

Chapter Five   33

Courage, Clarity, And Commitment   34

Chapter Six   41

Elevating Your Purpose Amid Challenges   42

Chapter Seven   49

Strength In Silence   50

Chapter Eight   57

Conquering Darkness   58

Chapter Nine   66

The Path To Greatness & Exceptional Living   67

Chapter Ten   73

Shine Forth   74

Chapter Eleven   81

Living With Purpose   82

Chapter Twelve   89

Power Keys To Rising And Staying Up   90

Chapter Thirteen   97

Power Keys To Rising, Staying Up And Shining Forth   98

Chapter Fourteen   105

Winning With God   106

Chapter Fifteen   112

Stand Out To Shine Forth   113

Chapter Sixteen   120

The Commanded Blessing   121

Chapter Seventeen   129

The Power Of The Blessing   130

Chapter Eighteen   135

Chapter Nineteen   142

The Power Of Divine Instructions   143

CONCLUSION   151

A SPECIAL CALL TO SALVATION & NEW BEGINNINGS   153
FROM APOSTLE DR. DAVID PHILEMON

ACKNOWLEDGMENTS

This book would not have been possible without the unwavering support, dedication, and talent of an extraordinary team. My deepest gratitude goes to each of you for your contributions, insights, and encouragement throughout this journey.

First and foremost, thank you to Rev. Mimi Philemon my dear wife, Rev. Shina Gentry, and and my assistant pastor Rev. Bright Amudoaghan for your incredible effort, encouragement, and belief in this project. Your support has been instrumental in bringing this vision to life.

To the dedicated leaders of Royal Diadem Publishing, Ide Imogie and Kishawna Bailey, I am immensely grateful for your belief in this project from the very beginning and for investing your time and energy into its development. Your creativity, dedication, and expertise have been the backbone of this endeavor.

I am especially grateful to the Royal Diadem Publishing team —Beulah Orogun, Emmanuella Ben-Eboh, Doyinsade Awodele, Kim Matthews, and Shante Gill, for your meticulous attention to detail, refining every page and ensuring that each word reflects our vision.

A heartfelt thank you to my family, friends, and colleagues whose unwavering support and belief in this project gave me the courage and strength to see it through.

Finally, thank you to all the readers and supporters who make this work meaningful. I am humbled and honored to share this journey with each of you.

With all my gratitude,
David Philemon

CHAPTER ONE

STRENGTH FOR DESTINY

S trength for destiny is not about brute force or the size of your muscles. It's something more profound and valuable; it is a resilience that speaks to your core and pushes you forward when others have already thrown the towel. When I talk of strength, I am not just talking about the ability to lift heavy things simply; I am talking about the power to lift yourself and others when the weight of life feels unbearable. You see true strength emerge when you believe in something bigger, something beyond the limitations of the moment, and something that doesn't just focus on you but on being a blessing to the world.

True strength is the faith that will carry you through the darkest nights when all logic says to quit and all signs point to defeat. You should know right now that this strength isn't loud or boastful; it doesn't need to prove itself because it knows it's rooted in something greater than circumstance.

Wisdom Capsules

1. "Strength is a vital component for the fulfillment of life's assignment and purpose." - ADP

2. "Strength is needed to possess your inheritance in God. - Obadiah 1:17. Your possession is your right - it is what God has kept for you." - ADP

3. "Strength is needed to respond to the call of God & destiny. - Judges 4:1-12. Do not relinquish your responsibility to another." - ADP

4. "Strength is needed to conceive and birth/deliver visions. - Hebrew 11:11 KJV. God wants to infuse into you strength beyond human strength for you to be able to conceive and discharge visions." - ADP

5. "Strength is needed to be permanently above your enemies. When you are above your enemies, you have dominion. You are permanently in charge. You are always smarter and ahead of your enemies. God has given you the strength. - Psalms 3:3; Ephesians 1:21 KJV" - ADP

6. "Strength is needed for life's accomplishments and winning life's battles. When God releases strength upon you, He enables you to pursue that assignment. - 1 Samuel 30:8 KJV" - ADP

7. "Secrets to connecting to the strength of God." - ADP

8. "The voice of God. - Psalm 29:4 KJV. When you hear the voice of God, you receive strength, and it makes you full of power." - ADP

9. "The revelational word of God. You can hear the voice of God from the Scriptures. As you stay in the word, you connect to the revelation word, which imparts strength. - Joshua 1:8; Genesis 1:1 KJV. When you connect to the word of God, you connect to strength - 1 John 2:14 KJV. Your greatest asset is the word of God - what makes you strong is the amount of word inside of

you." - ADP

10. "The power of the indwelling Holy Spirit. - Ephesians 3:16 KJV. The Spirit of God that dwells in you revitalizes your mortal body to enable you to rise above your enemies and fulfill destiny." - ADP

11. "The spirit of joyful songs. - Isaiah 12:3 KJV; Nehemiah 8:10 KJV" - ADP

12. "Joy is key to strength. Depression is access to weakness. People of songs are people of strength. - Psalm 118:14 KJV" - ADP

13. "Glory encounter service: faith is not an option if you want to stand strong. It is essential. - 1 John 5:4 KJV" - ADP

14. "To stand strong, diligently seek God by faith. Without a Holy Spirit-approved faith, you cannot make heaven. You must have a personal living active faith. - Romans 10:17 KJV" - ADP

15. "The only life that pleases God is the life that lives in the faith of God's words. What has God said about you?" - ADP

16. "The only way to stand upright with God is by faith. Faith is the principal thing. Get it!" - ADP

17. "Faith is like a fire that requires wood to burn. It is your responsibility to keep the flame burning and to keep feeding the flame." - ADP

18. "Faith can weaken, dissipate and evaporate from hearing the wrong words and from plain neglect." - ADP

19. "It is a dangerous thing to lose your faith. Peter began sinking because he ran out of gas (faith)." - ADP

20. "If you want to stand strong, put gas in your faith tank. Go to Jesus and replenish your faith before it runs out! - Hebrews 12:2 KJV. It takes more gas to go uphill than to go on level ground." - ADP

21. "There are some things in life that take more faith than others, and it can drain your faith tank very quickly." - ADP

22. "Never assume you have enough faith in your tank. Never let your tank go empty or run out of gas. Fill your faith tank always!" - ADP

23. "Concentrate on the word of God to build your faith. You will begin to sink once you take your eyes away from the word of God. Fill your faith tank always. - Proverbs 27:23 KJV" - ADP

24. "No matter what you have, be diligent. Always know the state of what you have and know when you need to replenish." - ADP

25. "You do not have to run out of gas. God has provided all you need to have a full tank and stand strong. All you need to do is listen to Him." - ADP

26. "Be aware of what you have. Take time to take care of what God has given to you. - Psalm 107:20 KJV" - ADP

27. "If you are running out of gas or getting weary, run back to the filling station - run back to the word of God." - ADP

28. "Faith can and should grow. It should be multiplying at all times." - ADP

29. "It does not matter how many times you have fallen; you can get back up and stand strong if you have a word to fill up your faith tank." - ADP

30. "No matter where the battle is coming from, just pull out faith from your faith tank and keep on going." - ADP

31. "Failure is only an event or a way out of life. Get up one more time. Do not stay down. Dust yourself up and keep on going. Finish strong no matter what the enemy says. Your best days are yet to come! - Micah 7:8 KJV" - ADP

32. "Learn how to walk by faith, not by sight." - ADP

33. "Do not get discouraged. When you fall, it is not the end. If it is not good news, it is not the last news." - ADP

34. "You may be in the midst of a storm thinking that people are watching you fight, struggle, or falter. You may think your faith is so weak, but that is a lie of the devil. You have an audience, and someone is watching you, taking notes of your feelings, and getting back up. Stay the course!" - ADP

35. "Resolve in your heart to stand strong no matter what the devil does." - ADP

36. "Stay the course! Stand strong! Keep your faith tank filled!" - ADP

CHAPTER TWO

THE BEST RESIDES IN YOU

Never let the world convince you that you are small or useless because when God created you, He infused you with unique qualities, talents, and a purpose that only you can fulfill. You see, each of us is designed intentionally, crafted with love and care. This means you are not a mistake but a masterpiece destined for greatness.

Accept the truth that God sees you as valuable and worthy. After accepting this truth, begin to see yourself the same way. When negative thoughts arise, remind yourself of your worth in Christ, realizing that Christ died for you and that you can achieve incredible things as long as you stay in him.

Child of God, stand firm in your identity; don't accept the labels life tries to place on you. Instead, celebrate your uniqueness and the gifts that you bring to the table.

You are unique and have everything it takes to make a difference.

Wisdom Capsules

1. "If you want to know where God is taking you, listen to what God is revealing to you." - ADP

2. "God shows you where He is taking you by the quality of revelation He makes available to you." - ADP

3. "God is drawn to radical people. Being radical means having a spirit that means you go against the tide. Being radical means knowing the heart of God and making up your mind to stand with God even if standing with God means standing alone." - ADP

4. "Prayer sustains everything. You do not have power if you have the Word but no prayer. You are simply a religious lecturer." - ADP

5. "Stop begging for people to like you. Start unlocking what is inside." - ADP

6. "God is putting you in a place where you will walk in the power of the Holy Spirit." - ADP

7. "God loves heights and loves those who are radical." - 2 Samuel 23:1-5 TLB - ADP

8. "Enter into an agreement with God that is eternal, final, and sealed." - ADP

9. "There is a share and a blessing with your name on it." - ADP

10. "The ridiculous is what releases the miraculous." - ADP

11. "Your greatest power is determined by your spirit to connect with spirits and have spirits recognize you as one. This is obtained in the place of prayer." - ADP

12. "Your inability to access what God has for you can enslave you under who God never intended for you to serve. A child of God can live like a slave and a loser, especially if that child of God is unable to access what God has for them." - ADP

13. "No matter how spiritual you are, until you come to a place where your spirituality gives you an upper hand, you will always be a slave to the one with the upper hand. There is a place of serving and a place of slavery. You will not be a slave!" - ADP

14. "If you do not have the money of life, you are considered poor. If you are poor until you do something about the poverty, you will always be ruled by the rich." - Proverbs 22:7 TPT/AMPC/ERV - ADP

15. "You will be the head and not the tail. In the name of Jesus." - Deuteronomy 28:12-13 TLB - ADP

16. "A person who ignores the need to master the art of consistency will be poor and be a loser. You must have the ability to be a finisher and be consistent." - ADP

17. "The way you think affects your future. You can be at the corridor of grace and glory and still be starved of blessings." - ADP

18. "Dream it. Frame it. Cream it. Claim it. Birth/manifest it." - ADP

19. "God wants you to own everything He gives to you." - ADP

20. "You must develop the capacity to run the magnitude of the blessing you have been praying for to receive the blessing God has for you." - ADP

21. "You must enlarge and elevate your level in your thoughts. Make power moves that will glorify God!" - ADP

22. "Give God the gift of a radical mindset, and you will find yourself standing tall!" - ADP

23. "If God is giving you cities, you must give Him

capacity." - ADP

24. "Withstanding tall comes greater responsibility, which is why God takes the time to process you so that you do not look at a city and sink under the weight of running it." - ADP

25. "God will not give you cities without giving you resources to run the cities successfully." - ADP

26. "What is faith? Faith is an expression of confidence in God and His Word." - ADP

27. "Faith is knowing what God wants and doing it by faith." - ADP

28. "Faith is knowing what God is saying and doing what God is saying." - ADP

29. "Faith is total submission to the power of God using the weapon of obedience to unlock the miracles no one expects you can have." - Hebrews 11:32-33 TPT - ADP

30. "Things are assigned to pull you down and stop you. You must seek out things that give you spiritual advantage." - ADP

31. "Do not allow the enemy to clog your heart with all the distractions that you are not able to hear your specific instructions." - ADP

32. "Specific divine instructions may be ridiculous or hard, but the ridiculous unlocks the miraculous. The power is in the details." - ADP

33. "There is no one that has ever been destroyed by Satan or any man without being allowed to find or create a way of escape. No one has ever risen in the Kingdom of God to become a shining star without finding out specific instructions. You only fly by instruction." -

ADP

34. "Most times, the greatness God ordained for people is harnessed in one word. But when the one word is ignored, 100 words can no longer solve that problem." - ADP

35. "No one ever successfully walks with God without pain or paying a high price." - ADP

36. "The beauty of a high price is that whenever high prices are paid, great destinies are unlocked, and the rise of the one that pays the price becomes unstoppable." - ADP

37. "Do you have a desire or determination to see God bring to pass what He had in mind for you? What are the specific instructions that you are running with?" - ADP

38. "God wants that instead of you begging Him for a miracle, you ask Him for an instruction. There is nothing you need from God that is not wrapped up in an instruction." - ADP

39. "You can run by discipline. You can drive by direction. But you run best by instruction." - ADP

40. "Distress is a spiritual alarm within your soul that tells you that danger has come or is coming. It is a divine alarm in a human being." - ADP

41. "When you begin to feel distressed, do not ignore it. It means that an evil, wrong, and foul spirit is knocking on your door or invading the atmosphere." - ADP

42. "Our highest need today is security. You have to be protected." - ADP

43. "The covenant secures that which we have. The

invisible world is seeking to dominate this world." - Proverbs 4:16 TLB; Jeremiah 6:14 KJV - ADP

44. "Many want what God has but do not want to know what it takes. God is seeking men and women who are hungry to know what the price is." - ADP

45. "You can walk in the fullness of God's favor, power, provision, and abundance blessings if you seek to know what it takes." - ADP

46. "It is a sin against destiny to ignore the salvation of your family." - ADP

47. "God is telling the church to build an ark! So, no matter how tough the flood is from the pit of hell, it cannot penetrate. Build your ark now with the right instructions. Do it right!" - ADP

48. "Trust God even when you do not see what you are told afore time." - Hebrews 11:7 ERV - ADP

49. "When God gives instructions, we look for the details. In looking for the details, God is pleased when He finds a man who wants to know what is next, how to handle next, and what to do about things." - ADP

50. "Whenever God warns you, your inaction reveals to God that you do not believe and you do not have faith in Him." - ADP

CHAPTER THREE

NAVIGATING SPIRITUAL INSTRUCTIONS & EMBRACING GOD'S GUIDELINES FOR SUCCESS

Success is something many people pursue, but true success, the kind that lasts and satisfies, can only be found in following God's instructions and embracing His guidelines for your life. I tell you the truth: when you neglect divine instructions or choose to walk your path, refusing to accept instruction from those who have gone ahead of you, I can tell you that no matter how far you think you have come, you will find yourself lost. The Bible clearly states that God has provided guidelines to help you steer through life effectively. But do you know what? You must intentionally choose to be obedient, stay in faith, and decide to trust the Lord.

One of the biggest mistakes you can make is thinking that you can figure out life on your own. Proverbs 3:5 says, *"Trust in the LORD with all thine heart, and lean not unto thine own understanding."* Why? Because your understanding is limited and flawed, but God's wisdom is perfect and boundless. God sees the beginning from the end and knows the best path for you, so trying to handle things your way or relying solely on human logic will only lead to confusion, frustration, and eventual failure.

Child of God, every command He gives you is for your benefit; they are not to make life harder but to make life more prosperous and more meaningful, so it's essential to examine your heart today.

Wisdom Capsules

1. "One of the worst things Satan can do to you is to put sickness in your children or grandchildren's body to mock you." - ADP

2. "What instructions are you holding on to? What are some instructions you have ignored, missed, or messed up? With God, there are fundamentals." - ADP

3. "God has your blessings that He wants to give you. Do not hold back and do not take from His own. Do not steal from God!" - ADP

4. "Mammon is a spirit. It will attack your mind until it justifies your disobedience so that it can ruin your destiny." - ADP

5. "Money is fundamental." - ADP

6. "A person shows his or her level of submission to Christ not by how many hours you pray or how many souls you win, but by how much money you part with in serving God." - Luke 21:1-4 ERV - ADP

7. "The power of the sacrifice is so powerful that things we call normal, God calls fundamental." - ADP

8. "A believer begins to fall when he/she starts negotiating giving." - ADP

9. "Hell checks out your strength in the spirit realm. Your level of investment!" - ADP

10. "When you master a little instruction, God shows you giant strides. Ask God to correct and direct you. Ask Him to show you the steps to take." - ADP

11. "Do not follow your head or your heart. Your head and your heart can deceive you. Follow the charted directions - it is called divine instructions." - ADP

12. "Do not claim to know it. Ask, 'Lord, show me.'" - Psalm 25:10 MSG - ADP

13. "Declare this: I am an arrow. I am God's arrow targeted to hit giants. I am an arrow, and I will hit God's bullseye." - Psalm 25:13-14 MSG - ADP

14. "A divine season without the factor of favor leads to a crippled destiny no matter how great that destiny seems. When favor is limited, wretchedness is increased." - ADP

15. "When the devil desires to attack a person, he releases the spirit of the tail. His goal is to take the person from being the head to being the tail. The spirit of the tail constantly empowers the dragon to eat that which is being birthed." - ADP

16. "The highest unlocker of HIGH FAVOR is spiritual fervency. When spiritual fervency begins to decrease, favor begins to dry. Never allow the devil to negotiate God's position in your life." - ADP

17. "The more powered your destiny is, the greater use you are to mankind." - ADP

18. "Satan brings forth lies to pull down stars. When Satan brings a lie to your mind, either he brings a false prophet or

makes you a false prophet to yourself to use as the tail to pull you down." - ADP

19. "High favor gives you the wisdom to access what people with just favor cannot access. Favor that brings wealth only is not enough to secure happiness." - ADP

20. "If you want to command high favor and high respect from God, you must be in a sincere partnership with God to the point that you are willing to let Him know that everything that comes through you belongs to Him." - ADP

21. "When the favor of God is in search of a candidate, it looks for those who truly connect with Him with intentionality." - ADP

22. "When you desire to advance in the Kingdom of God, your motives will be tested. No obstacle will be strong enough to block you if your motives are pure. The highest honor of life comes when life is lived for the purpose in which life was given." - ADP

23. "True perfection is when one gives himself and aligns with God's perfection. High favor does not come by simply desiring or wishing for it... High favor is obtained by sacrifice." - ADP

24. "To fulfill high-level destiny, you need high favor, not limited favor. If your purpose is high, then you need high favor. If your purpose is low, you can apply for a higher assignment and position yourself for high favor so you can fulfill the high assignment." - ADP

25. "God wants you to live with a sense of purpose. You must live life obsessed with the divine assignment given to you. The sooner you secure God's high favor, the better!" - ADP

26. "For God to leave the mark of His presence with a person, He leaves His high favor. Favor is one of the practical evidence that God is with a person." - ADP

27. "Favor will cause you to achieve in a short time what many can't achieve in a lifetime. Favor makes life's journey not just easier but worth it." - ADP

28. "If the price of the assignment or destiny is normal, then the favor derived is not high. High favor comes at a high cost, and it has no expiration date." - ADP

29. "The favor God gives depends on the assignment's generosity. God gives high favor with the mindset of it being used for His highest glory. When God gives a person high favor, He lifts the person high in life." - ADP

30. "The height you are willing to rise to in life is determined by the sacrifice you are willing to make for the honor of your life." - ADP

31. "The Spirit of high favor comes when God finds a heart or a soul that is sincerely longing to partner with Him." - ADP

32. "To obtain high favor, DISCOVER your God-given potential - MINE (Develop) your God-given potential - DEPLOY your God-given potential. Raise the standard for yourself. The responsibility is on you!" - ADP

33. "To obtain high favor, be a high-level visionary thinker. Think against your weaknesses. Think impossible thoughts. Let your thoughts create vision. The more you think, the more power you generate. The more you think higher, the more you connect with divine ability, capacity, and capability." - Ephesians 3:20 - ADP

34. "Raise the standard for yourself so that people will think you have lost your mind. Nobody will develop you for you." - ADP

35. "Do not think depressing thoughts. The worst thing you can do when you find yourself in a pit is to continue digging. Think your way out of the pit. There is something magnetic about your thoughts!" - ADP

36. "The hunger and desire of man brings forth honor. So when you run out of water, do not die. Switch your thinking and begin to think of what can be done with that which you have." - ADP

37. "When God desires to do high things in your life, He creates wells in the wilderness. Think according to the high vision, not your resources. God will always create a well when all you need is a bottle. Don't ever dream based on your resources, and do not think according to your limitations. Think according to your divine vision. It will attract resources." - ADP

38. "Any individual who intentionally decides to diligently pursue God's purpose for their life and their generation will always unlock high favor. High favor is unlocked by an intentional desire and discipline to apply diligence in the pursuit of God for their life and humanity." - ADP

39. "People who embrace diligence end up men and women of high dignity. Be diligent in seeking God and in executing assignments. Make up your mind to not give excuses on why things are not working." - ADP

40. "High strength comes from the Most High God. If everything God demands from you can be accomplished by the strength you have, then you are regarded as a low favor carrier because every high assignment requires high strength." - ADP

41. "Anyone lazy pursuing destiny will become enslaved forever. Anyone who succeeds needs strength. The strength of God must supersede yours." - ADP

42. "If you dream beyond your strength, favor steps in, and the moment favor steps in, all of a sudden, God begins to show things and do things with you that will surprise you." - ADP

43. "Grow your oil...it empowers. When the anointing comes on a person's head, the strength of God becomes the strength of the man, and the diligence required will be applied not because

of the man's strength but because of the strength of God." - Proverbs 12:24 KJV - ADP

44. "Check your associations. Relationships are important, but toxic relationships are dangerous. Disloyalty is the quickest killer of oil. Association affects your acceleration to the right destination." - ADP

45. "When you find yourself, know your level. Closeness to God will remove the darkness. When you're close to God, you hardly miss anything." - ADP

46. "To operate in high favor, you must humble yourself before your calling. Rising to the top is easier and faster if your father opens the door for you." - ADP

47. "The greatest secret is closeness to God. If you are close to God, He will always interpret things to you. If you desire to be great, talk to God. How can you be a stranger to God and hear him all the time." -ADP

CHAPTER FOUR

COURAGEOUS FAITH & UNLOCKING YOUR PATH TO SUCCESS AND FAVOR

Courageous faith is one of the keys to unlocking the success and favors God has planned for your life. Now, you need to know that it takes more than passive belief to fulfill God's promises; it requires bold and courageous action. The life of Joshua in the Bible is a prime example of this principle. After Moses' death, God called Joshua to lead the Israelites into the Promised Land. This was no small task; it was filled with battles, challenges, and uncertainties, yet God repeatedly commanded Joshua to be "strong and of good courage" (Joshua 1:6-9). Why? Because courageous faith was necessary for him to succeed.

The same is true for you; without courage, it is impossible to step into the life God has for you entirely. There will be times when God asks you to move into the unknown, to take steps that seem risky, and to trust Him even when the circumstances are overwhelming. That's where faith comes in. Courageous faith is not the absence of fear but the willingness to act despite fear, knowing that God is with you and will guide you to victory.

Many times, people fail to experience the fullness of God's favor and success because they stop short at the edge of faith. Fear holds them back, doubt creeps in, and they miss the blessings from stepping out in faith. Look at Joshua again; he had to lead the people across the Jordan River, conquer fortified cities like Jericho, and face powerful enemies. None of this was easy, but his courage came from the confidence that God was with him. He knew that success wasn't dependent on his abilities but on God's power.

Wisdom Capsules

1. "Spiritual Sensitivity is key! You cannot be noisy in your soul and be a success in your spiritual journey. Study to be quiet." - 1 Thessalonians 4:11 - ADP

2. "Be strong and courageous. Courage is the conqueror's backbone. It gives way to success." - ADP

3. "Courage is not the absence of fear but the ability to measure your fear and summon courage to back it up. If you are courageous, it will pave the way to success. Winners never quit, and quitters never win." - ADP

4. "When you are dependable, whatever is entrusted into your care will be counted on to produce results. Many people cannot access their possessions because they are unreliable." - Proverbs 25:19 TPT - ADP

5. "Faithfulness is being constant in and out of season. It is the ability to make your life assignment the priority of your living; God will not instruct you beyond the level of your last obedience. It is required in stewardship that a man be found faithful." - ADP

6. "Faithfulness is a thing of the soul and heart. When God finds an imperfect but faithful man, He is drawn to them. Competence

and perfection can be taught." - ADP

7. "Failed yesterday? Try again today - Win tomorrow. Turn your past failures to God. Build your self-confidence." - ADP

8. "Gratitude is a key to happiness. It makes you stay happy. Ingratitude will make you forget what kept you for up to a decade. It will make you forget the benefits you have experienced." - 2 Sam 21:17 - ADP

9. "Favor removes the fight from your life without you missing the flight of your life. Show me a grateful person, and I will show you a highly favored one who will be a possessor of the west and south." - ADP

10. "Passion without focus is a disaster waiting to happen. Do not trade your destiny moment for personal pleasure." - ADP

11. "Gratitude makes you interpret things right. It makes you value the strength that made you strong, the wisdom that made you wise, the power that made you powerful, the covering that covered you from the pestilence and arrows from the enemy, the holiness that made you holy, the consecration that made you concentrated, the discipline that showed you how to be disciplined, the diligence that inspired you to make you more diligent, the vision that made you a visionary, the passion that ignited your passion, and the focus that focused your passion." - ADP

12. "Great meetings do not make great men, but great decisions make great men." - ADP

13. "Every time you sow the seed of favor, you will command the harvest of high favor. A good man who will always show favor will become a magnet of favor." - ADP

14. "When an irritation from hell is not tamed, the next thing Satan brings is revenge. Irritation comes to test your new authority." - ADP

15. "God tests you; Satan tempts you. Tests come to bring you promotion; temptation comes to entrap you." - ADP

16. "When interpreting life, you must interpret it through the lens of purpose. Do not go on a spiritual vacation. Ask yourself why am I here?" - ADP

17. "You must embrace the ability to receive from God, retain what has been received, and multiply what has been retained. Otherwise, Satan will try to take you back to where you used to be." - ADP

18. "If you are not practically involved with life, life will outrun you." - ADP

19. "Hate mediocrity, spiritual uselessness, and lack of spiritual ranking. Refuse to be the party house of demons by engaging yourself in the things of God." - Luke 11:25-26 TLB - ADP

20. "Holiness, purity, and prosperity attract demons. Whenever you do not use your holiness, purity, and prosperity for the advancement of the Kingdom of God, demons are coming for you." - ADP

21. "Demons are coming back for anyone who will not do anything with the encounters and visitation given to them." - ADP

22. "Many believers do not hold on to encounters, and they become victims of the demons they once defeated. The only way to win is to endure to the end." - Hebrews 2:1; Hebrews 10:23 KJV - ADP

23. "Spiritual things are slippery if you do not hold on to what you have received well. Take your spirituality with you wherever you go." - ADP

24. "Spiritual grounds are also slippery. God makes the path your enemies take to attack you slippery. You will never attain a

height and fall from that height." - ADP

25. "The purpose of freedom is more conquest. The reason God sets you free and enlarges your coast/territory is not so that you relax but so that you can fight and win some more." - Psalm 17:4 TPT - ADP

26. "The chariot wheels of God move with precision and without mistake. They carry the thrones of God. The chariot wheels of God guarantee that you will begin to live life with almost absolute precision — a realm of superhuman strength." - Psalm 17:5 TPT - ADP

27. "Anointing coupled with intelligence equals EXCELLENCE. Anointing should never be a substitute for intelligence." - ADP

28. "Stay on course on the path of greatness. Don't lose what you have labored for. It costs too much. You will never stray." - ADP

29. "Everything you capture has a future. When you hunt, you capture and nurture so that you can protect your future." - ADP

30. "If you are going to attract God, you must know that you are sent." - ADP

31. "The high places of the earth are not for wimps, lazy people, or those looking for their lucky day. It is for those who are willing to fight for their trophy." - ADP

32. "When a person masters how the earth works, he/she will occupy the high places of the earth. Study the system — Be diligent — Embrace the anointing and understand how the earth works, then work it God's way." - ADP

33. "The matters of our days must be solved by men with hearts, not by men with heads." - Isaiah 44:25 - ADP

34. "Do not compromise your path to greatness. Your faithfulness will always generate greatness." - ADP

35. "It is an insult to God's anointing to have oil on your head and not run over." - ADP

36. "We do not win when we do things our way. We win when we do things God's way. This is the realm that makes you take over." - ADP

37. "The lessons you dodge today will create your warfare tomorrow." - ADP

38. "Do not be in a hurry to show off. In life, there is a season of incubation. When the season of incubation matures, it leads to a season of manifestation. Respect your season of incubation!" - ADP

39. "Your relationship with the King of Zion will determine your confidence in taking your place, just like Daniel. Align with God." - ADP

40. "When there is no incubation, manifestation ends up in disaster. Your prophecy is aching for its manifestation. Don't despise the process." - ADP

41. "Every time you dodge the training of God, you sabotage your reigning in life." - ADP

42. "High favor comes at a high cost, but when you pay the price, you have the right to erupt like a volcano." - ADP

43. "Divinely defining moments is a combination of several moments to help you create momentum that will help you attain your promised future." - ADP

44. "Everyone that encounters Christ Jesus with an open heart and mind has a change of story to tell. It is the right of everyone to expect changes from God. God wants you to be expectant and intentional about what you will do with the changes and upgrades He brings into your life." - ADP

45. "If you sit on a glory so big without spreading it to the world,

it begins to shrink. Experience the Power that allows you to go across the globe and disseminate/express the Power and Glory of God through your life." - ADP

46. "As a representative of God, you are required to be productive. Every crisis has a solution. Do not let your challenges intimidate or insult you." - ADP

47. "Do not allow adversity to become the end of your life's journey. Adversity/hostility comes to test your authenticity. By all means, ensure that you end up with prosperity!" - ADP

48. "KHAYIL is the power that enables you to generate ideas and convert them into substance — something practical." - Psalm 110:3 (AMP) - ADP

49. "GADOL is the power of progress. It is the power that inflates your efforts. It announces and gets attention for itself." - ADP

50. "GADOL comes like a volcanic eruption. It explodes from the inside and makes the needed noise. It bursts forth like fire and melts anything that cannot stand its presence. When it settles, it reveals its glory. It births a new level of honor and respect." - ADP

51. "The capacity to develop GADOL in your life can change your entire life. Do not ignore your passion and your greatest source of life. GADOL will always announce its presence." - ADP

52. "When you cultivate the 'fruit' of your GADOL, people will recognize you. You will take a place of significance. You will be remembered." - ADP

53. "Unveil the qualities of your KHAYIL and GADOL and pursue them fiercely. Do not rest until they become a lifestyle. When they do, they will not just be talents. They will be skills that produce substance." - ADP

54. "God knows when you are struggling with skills. The greater the pressure, the greater the essence He needs to draw out of

you." - ADP

55. "You were built to take advantage of the adversity around you to show the world the level of glory and presence of God in you." - ADP

56. "The presence of God is what gives you KHAYIL. Your greatest pursuit in life is to pursue God." - ADP

57. "What you do not focus on, you do not become." - ADP

58. "Keep focusing on your focus until the season of your victory breaks forth." - ADP

59. "No one conquers from behind; everyone conquers from the front." - ADP

60. "The word 'victory' is a thought process." - ADP

61. "No man ever loses in life unless he loses faith in himself." - ADP

62. "Don't let your human limitations limit you! Let the Holy Spirit empower you." - ADP

63. "The possibility of failure must never determine how you advance towards greatness." - ADP

64. "Your triumph begins in your ability to dream and envision yourself in the future. Let that vision stay with you and propel you to your destination." - ADP

65. "Eagle anointing is a lifetime of change. It produces generational blessings." - ADP

66. "Excellence is the ability to keep your dream alive. No matter what happens, the thought of your dream must always be with you." - ADP

67. "The biggest mistake anyone can make is to underestimate themselves." - ADP

68. "No one has ever gotten tired of chasing what they believe in." - ADP

69. "Only God can help you see the whole picture. It is not every time you will know where you are going, but you will know who is with you." - ADP

70. "Every time you experience a change, let it be a change that advances you into God's plan." - ADP

71. "Your story must not die, your purpose must not die, your legacy must not die, your family must not die." - ADP

72. "Dreams become great because they are linked to the greatness of God." - ADP

73. "Your lifestyle must never deny your dreams." - ADP

74. "You are equipped for greatness." - ADP

75. "What you can't see, you cannot take." - ADP

76. "God wants you to have the best and be the best." - ADP

77. "Know your worth; understand how valuable you are." - ADP

78. "Be unapologetic for who you are." - ADP

79. "Every encounter with God is a turning point for your life. Make it count!" - ADP

80. "You are a product of the choices you make." - ADP

81. "The trajectory of your future is dependent on the decisions you make in the present." - ADP

82. "Life has no restrictions; the only restrictions are the limitations you place on yourself." - ADP

83. "When God lifts you up, do not put your mouth on others who are down." - ADP

84. "You can't fulfill God's assignment without God." - ADP

85. "You are designed to win." - ADP

86. "You are empowered to create solutions." - ADP

87. "You are loaded with potentials, and the Holy Spirit wants to help you to manifest those potentials." - ADP

88. "The kind of life you want is within your grasp." - ADP

89. "Do not be afraid of who you were born to be." - ADP

90. "Be diligent and dedicated to the pursuit of your dreams." - ADP

91. "Don't hide your greatness. Don't hide your testimony. Let the world see what God can do!" - ADP

92. "Be a conduit of blessings." - ADP

93. "In the economy of God, nothing goes wasted. The same power that raised Jesus from the dead is inside of you." - ADP

94. "Your moment of greatness will happen. It is inevitable." - ADP

95. "Your testimony is not about you. It is about what God can do through you." - ADP

96. "Every trial is a chance for you to shine." - ADP

97. "Your courage is a seed of change." - ADP

98. "Let God order your steps." - ADP

99. "Your story is a legacy of faith." - ADP

100. "Be a force for good in the world." – ADP

CHAPTER FIVE

COURAGE, CLARITY, AND COMMITMENT

*Keys to Achieving Your
Divine Destiny*

Fulfilling your God-given destiny requires three critical elements, which are "courage, clarity, and commitment". Well, each of these aspects plays a vital role in ensuring that you walk in the purpose for which you were created. You must know and never forget that you are not here by accident; God has a plan for your life; I am talking about a unique destiny that only you can fulfill. But walking in that purpose isn't always easy, and it requires more than just a desire; it requires bold action, a clear vision, and an unshakable level of dedication toward your life and destiny.

Let's start with **courage**: To fulfill your destiny, you must step into the unknown and trust God with your future. This is very essential because fear will always try to hold you back. When God called Jeremiah, He told him not to be afraid of the faces of the people (Jeremiah 1:8), knowing that fear could stop him from fulfilling his prophetic role. You too will face moments of fear and doubt as you pursue your purpose so know that there will be opposition, challenges, and even failures along the way, but courage will allow you to move forward in faith despite these obstacles. Yes, you must be willing to step out even when you don't have all the answers or when the path seems difficult.

Let's talk about **clarity**: Without a clear understanding of God's purpose for your life, you will wander. But how will you get clarity, clarity comes from seeking God through prayer, studying His Word, and listening to His voice. You cannot fulfill a destiny that you are unclear about, Jeremiah knew exactly what God had called him to do because God made it clear to him "I ordained thee a prophet unto the nations" (Jeremiah 1:5). You need that same clarity about your purpose. What has God called you to do? What are the gifts and talents He has placed in you to fulfill that purpose? Clarity brings focus, and focus brings progress.

Now on **commitment:** Commitment is the anchor that keeps you grounded in the pursuit of your destiny; it is not enough to start well; you must be willing to finish strong, and this is why commitment means sticking with God's plan even when things get tough. It's easy to be enthusiastic at the beginning of your journey, but the real test comes when you face delays, disappointments, and difficulties. Will you still be committed to God's purpose when the path gets rocky? Will you continue to trust Him when things don't go as planned? These are the questions you must answer if you want to go far.

Wisdom Capsules

1. "Dream Big — Imagine Big — Execute Big." - ADP

2. "God wants you to fulfill your purpose for your life. The wicked will do everything to neutralize you. If you are going to overcome the spirit of envy, you must tame or defeat it." - ADP

3. "Envy is the disregard for the process or price someone else paid for their greatness. Envy is the express license to work with Satan. Examine your heart!" - ADP

4. "The most important thing in life is why life was given to you. Every relationship must center around the purpose for which you are living." - ADP

5. "Revelation without Power to change the lives of others only makes you a lecturer." - ADP

6. "The spirit of envy, when the Power of God does not tame it, Kills— Deprives— Robs— and Destroys." - ADP

7. "When Satan inspires you to envy others, he is programming you for disaster. When you act on behalf of Satan, you program yourself for defeat." - ADP

8. "Disconnect yourself from the mysticism that controls life. REFUSE TO FAIL!" - ADP

9. "If Your Greatness Cannot Inspire Me, Why Should Your Smallness Expire Me?" - ADP

10. "The Power of God makes you a distributor for God. Power with God makes you a bonafide Partner." - ADP

11. "Declare your new status. Say 'BECAUSE I HAVE BEEN STRONG WITH GOD, I WILL PREVAIL WITH MEN. IN JESUS NAME. AMEN' - Genesis 32:28 TLB" - ADP

12. "Daydream + Imagination + Diligence + Consistency = THE BEST DREAM. Talent + Discipline = EXCELLENCE." - ADP

13. "A divine season without the factor of favor leads to a crippled destiny no matter how great that destiny seems. When favor is limited, wretchedness is increased." - ADP

14. "When the devil desires to attack a person, he releases the spirit of the tail. His goal is to take the person from being the head to being the tail. The spirit of the tail constantly empowers the dragon to eat that which is being birthed." - ADP

15. "The highest unlocker of HIGH FAVOR is Spiritual Fervency.

When spiritual fervency begins to decrease, favor begins to dry. Never allow the devil to negotiate God's position in your life." - ADP

16. "The more powered your destiny is, the greater use you are to mankind." - ADP

17. "Satan brings forth lies to pull down stars. When Satan brings a lie to your mind, either he brings a false prophet or makes you a false prophet to yourself to use as the tail to pull you down." - ADP18. "High-Favor gives you the wisdom to access what people with Just-Favor cannot access. Favor that brings wealth only is not enough to secure happiness." - ADP

19. "If you want to command high favor and high respect from God, you must be in a sincere partnership with God to the point that you are willing to let Him know that everything that comes through you belongs to Him." - ADP

20. "When the favor of God is in search of a candidate, it looks for those who truly connect with him with intentionality." - ADP

21. "When you desire to advance in the Kingdom of God, your motives will be tested. If your motives are pure, no obstacle will be strong enough to block you. The highest honor of life comes when life is lived for the purpose in which life was given." - ADP

22. "True Perfection is when one gives himself and aligns with God's Perfection. High favor does not come by simply desiring or wishing for it...High Favor is obtained by sacrifice." - ADP

23. "To fulfill high-level destiny, you need High-Favor, not limited favor. If your purpose is high, then you need high favor. If your purpose is low, you can apply for a higher assignment and position yourself for high favor so you can fulfill the high assignment." - ADP

24. "God wants you to live with a sense of purpose. You must live life obsessed with the divine assignment given to you. The

sooner you secure God's high favor, the better!" - ADP

25. "For God to leave the mark of His presence with a person, He leaves His High Favor. Favor is one of the practical evidences that God is with a person." - ADP

26. "Favor will cause you to achieve in a short time what many can't achieve in a lifetime. Favor makes life's journey easier and worth it." - ADP27. "If the price of the assignment or destiny is normal, then the favor derived is not high. High favor comes at a high cost and it has no expiration date." - ADP

28. "The favor God gives is dependent on the magnanimity of the assignment. God gives high favor with the mindset of it being used for His highest glory. When God gives a person high favor, he lifts the person high in life." - ADP

29. "The height you are willing to rise to in life is determined by the sacrifice you are willing to make for the honor of your life." - ADP

30. "The Spirit Of High Favor comes when God finds a heart or a soul that is sincerely longing to partner with Him." - ADP

31. "To obtain High Favor, DISCOVER your God-given potential - MINE (Develop) your God-given potential - DEPLOY your God-given potential. Raise the standard for yourself. The responsibility is on you!" - ADP

32. "To obtain High Favor, be a high-level visionary thinker. Think against your weaknesses. Think impossible thoughts. Let your thoughts create vision. The more you think, the more power you generate. The more you think higher, the more you connect with divine ability, capacity and capability." - Ephesians 3:20 - ADP

33. "Raise the standard for yourself in such a way that people will think you have lost your mind. Nobody will develop you for you." - ADP

34. "Do not think depressing thoughts. The worst thing you can do when you find yourself in a pit is to continue digging. Think your way out of the pit. There is something magnetic about your thoughts!" - ADP

35. "The hunger and desire of man brings forth honor. So when you run out of water, do not die. Switch your thinking and begin to think of what can be done with that which you have." - ADP

36. "When God desires to do high things in your life, he creates wells in the wilderness. Think according to the high vision, not your resources. God will always create a well when all you need is a bottle. Don't ever dream based on your resources and do not think according to your limitations. Think according to your divine vision. It will attract resources." - ADP

37. "Any individual who intentionally decides to be diligent in the pursuit of God's purpose for their life and for their generation will always unlock High Favor. High Favor is unlocked by an intentional desire and discipline to apply diligence in the pursuit of God for the purpose of their life and humanity." - ADP

38. "People who embrace diligence end up men and women of high dignity. Be diligent in seeking God and in executing assignments. Make up your mind to not give excuses on why things are not working." - ADP

39. "High strength comes from the Most High God. If everything God demands from you can be accomplished by the strength you have, then you are regarded as a low favor carrier because every high assignment requires high strength." - ADP

40. "Anyone who is lazy in the pursuit of destiny will become a slave forever. Anyone who succeeds needs strength. The strength of God must supersede yours." - ADP

41. "If you dream beyond your strength, favor steps in and the

moment favor steps in, all of a sudden, God begins to show things and do things with you that will surprise you." - ADP

42. "Grow your oil...it empowers. When the anointing comes on a person's head, the strength of God becomes the strength of the man and the diligence required will be applied not because of the man's strength but because of the strength of God." - Proverbs 12:24 KJV - ADP

43. "Check your associations. Relationships are important but toxic relationships are dangerous. Disloyalty is the quickest killer of oil. Association affects your acceleration to the right destination." - ADP

44. "When you find yourself, know your level. Closeness to God will remove the darkness. When you're close to God, you hardly miss anything." - ADP

45. "To operate in high favor, you must totally humble yourself before your calling. Rising to the top is easier and faster if your father opens the door for you." - ADP

46. "The greatest secret is closeness to God. If you are close to God, He will always interpret things to you. If you desire to be great, talk to God. How can you be a stranger to God and hear him all the time? It is impossible." - ADP

CHAPTER SIX

ELEVATING YOUR PURPOSE AMID CHALLENGES

"The Power Of Faith And Favor"

C hallenges are inevitable when you pursue your God-given purpose because life's difficulties can sometimes seem overwhelming, but with faith in God and His favor surrounding you, no obstacle is insurmountable. Faith gives you the strength to push through challenges, while God's favor opens doors and provides opportunities that otherwise seem impossible. Think about the life of Joseph. Despite the many challenges he faced, he was betrayed by his brothers, sold into slavery, and falsely accused, Joseph never lost sight of God's purpose for his life.

His life was full of setbacks, but his faith remained steadfast; even when his circumstances seemed hopeless, Joseph believed that God's hand was still guiding him. As a result, God's favor was with Joseph in every situation. Genesis 39:2-3 says, "And the LORD was with Joseph, and he was a prosperous man; and he was in the house of his master the Egyptian." Even as a slave in Potiphar's house, God's favor caused Joseph to rise to a position of authority.

The favor of God doesn't always remove you from challenges, but it elevates you amid them; just like Joseph, you may be in a difficult place today, whether it's a tough job, a strained relationship, or a personal struggle, nevertheless, I want you to know that with faith in God and His favor on your life, those challenges will not destroy your destiny. Instead, they will refine you and position you for greater things.

Wisdom Capsules

1. "Greatness is magnetic, not repellant. Greatness attracts great people. If the power you possess is not powerful enough to power your favor, then you are small." - ADP

2. "Fathers provide divine covering. They transfer covenant to their sons and daughters. Covenant in the spirit realm is an elevator, not a mere ladder." - ADP

3. "Yes, life is a battlefield but divine favor turns your battlefield into your playground." - ADP

4. "When your favor is decreasing, your feet will reflect it by the places you enter. An unfavored life leads you to barren ground but a favored life leads you to wealthy places." - Proverbs 4:18 - ADP

5. "Arrogance and self-sufficiency paralyze the flow of favor." - ADP

6. "God's word describes your reality. When wisdom marries understanding, they both give birth to favor." - ADP

7. "When you understand, you see and interpret correctly; but when you apply that understanding, then you are wise. Wisdom is applied revelation and understanding. A wise man will always attract favor!" - ADP

8. "You can achieve a lot of things with your hard work, but favor adds flavor to a man's labor. Disfavor makes your labor seem

senseless." - ADP

9. "Be fruitful (bring value), multiply, replenish the earth, and revalue it. Rebrand and recreate a new system of operation." - ADP

10. "Favor gives you access to everything needed to fulfill your prophecy. You are the answer to many unfulfilled prophecies." - Isaiah 45:4 - ADP

11. "Favor is not just a game changer but the game changer. It is the accelerator of destiny and a major key which gives you speed without the extraordinary struggle. When your life lacks favor, you struggle." - ADP

12. "Whenever God is doing anything in the lives of His people, He increases or expects to increase their favor." - ADP

13. "Someone holds what your destiny requires, and favor positions you to get it witlessly. Favor will cause others to do your dirty work and produce a beautiful outcome." - ADP

14. "God can turn your scars into stars, but favor makes you a star without the scars because someone will fight the fight and get the scar so that you can be the star." - ADP

15. "Favor makes you a star without the scars. It takes away the struggle needed for the destination you are traveling to. Favor turns you into an overnight success." - Isaiah 45:5 TLB - ADP

16. "One of the keys to receiving favor is releasing and sowing favor." - ADP

17. "Favor flows in the direction of mission and vision. It makes you a problem solver. Show me a mission and vision that is powered by passion, and I will show you a life that has uncommon favor." - ADP

18. "Favor leads to a life of accomplishment. Where favor is limited, flavor is limited and labor is abundant." - ADP

19. "Favor is magnetic in nature, not repellant. Favor attracts great people. Great minds attract great minds. If your favor is decreasing, your feet will reflect it by the places you go to." - ADP

20. "In life, it's better for a righteous man to slap you than a wicked person to kiss. But a kiss is sweeter than a slap, so you settle for a temporal kiss that will soon kill." - ADP

21. "Understanding gives you the right perspective; wisdom gives you the right application of life. Wisdom is the ability of what to do, when to do, and how to do. Wisdom gives you the ability to apply your understanding." - Matthew 7:24 KJV - ADP

22. "Wisdom is applied revelation and applied understanding. Understanding is looking from God's eyes and lens. Your situation does not define reality. God's word is what defines reality." - ADP

23. "Grow your understanding; good understanding procures favor. When favor loses viscosity, you need to increase it. When you apply spiritual principles, your favor gets stronger and stronger." - ADP

24. "The secret of your success is in the problems you solve. Solve less problems and you'll be less successful. Solve more problems and you'll be more successful. Solve many problems and you'll be extraordinarily successful." - ADP

25. "Spiritual sensitivity is key! You cannot be noisy in your soul and be a success in your spiritual journey. Study to be quiet." - 1 Thessalonians 4:11 - ADP

26. "Be strong and courageous. Courage is the conqueror's backbone. It gives way to success." - ADP

27. "Courage is not the absence of fear but the ability to measure your fear and summon courage to back it up. If you are courageous, it will pave the way to success. Winners never quit, and quitters never win." - ADP

28. "When you are dependable, whatever is entrusted into your care will be counted on to produce results. Many people cannot access the possessing of their possession because they are unreliable." - Proverbs 25:19 TPT - ADP

29. "Faithfulness is being constant in and out of season. It is the ability to make your life assignment the priority of your living. God will not instruct you beyond the level of your last obedience. It is required in stewardship that a man be found faithful." - ADP

30. "Faithfulness is a thing of the soul and heart. When God finds an imperfect but faithful man, He is drawn to them. Competence and perfection can be taught." - ADP

31. "Failed yesterday? Try again today - win tomorrow. Turn your past failures to God. Build your self-confidence." - ADP

32. "Gratitude is a key to happiness. It makes you stay happy. Ingratitude will make you forget what kept you for up to a decade. It will make you forget the benefits you have experienced." - 2 Samuel 21:17 - ADP

33. "Favor removes the fight from your life without you missing the flight of your life. Show me a grateful person and I will show you a highly favored one who will be a possessor of the west and south." - ADP

34. "Passion without focus is disaster waiting to happen. Do not trade your destiny moment for personal pleasure." - ADP

35. "Gratitude makes you interpret things right. It makes you value the strength that made you strong, the wisdom that made you wise, the power that made you powerful, the covering that covered you from the pestilence and arrows from the enemy, the holiness that made you holy, the consecration that made you concentrated, the discipline that showed you how to be disciplined, the diligence that inspired you to make you more

diligent, the vision that made you a visionary, the passion that ignited your passion, and the focus that focused your passion." - ADP

36. "Great meetings do not make great men, but great decisions make great men." - ADP

37. "Every time you sow the seed of favor, you will command the harvest of high favor. A good man who will always show favor will become a magnet of favor." - ADP

38. "Fill your faith tank always. No matter what you have, be diligent. Always know the state of what you have and know when to replenish." - ADP

39. "You do not have to run out of gas. God has provided all you need to have a full tank and stand strong. All you need to do is listen to Him." - ADP

40. "Be cognizant of what you have." - ADP

41. "Take time to take care of what God has given to you." - Psalm 107:20 KJV - ADP

42. "If you are running out of gas or getting weary, run back to the filling station - run back to the word of God." - ADP

43. "Faith can and should grow. It should be multiplying at all times." - ADP

44. "It does not matter how many times you have fallen down, you can get back up and stand strong if you have a word to fill up your faith tank. No matter where the battle is coming from, just pull out faith from your faith tank and keep on going." - ADP

45. "Failure is only an event. It is not a way out of life. Get up one more time, do not stay down." - ADP

46. "Dust yourself up and keep on going." - ADP

47. "Finish strong no matter what the enemy says. Your best days are yet to come!" - Micah 7:8 KJV - ADP

48. "Learn how to walk by faith, not by sight." - ADP

49. "Do not get discouraged. When you fall down, it is not the end. If it is not good news, it is not the last news." - ADP

50. "You may be in the midst of a storm thinking that people are watching you to fight, struggle or falter." - ADP

51. "You may think that your faith is so weak but that is a lie of the devil." - ADP

52. "You have an audience and someone out there is watching you and taking notes of how you fell and got back up. Stay the course!" - ADP

53. "Resolve in your heart to stand strong no matter what the devil does. Stay the course! Stand strong! Keep your faith tank filled!"

CHAPTER SEVEN

STRENGTH IN SILENCE

*Unlocking Your Voice And
Destiny In God*

In a world filled with noise and constant activity, it's easy to underestimate the power of silence. Yet, it is often in moments of quietness that God speaks the loudest and reveals the most amazing revelations about our lives and destiny. Silence isn't the absence of activity or progress; it is a place where strength is built, where you unlock your true voice, and where God prepares you for the journey ahead. Think about Elijah's experience in 1 Kings 19. After a great victory on Mount Carmel, Elijah was discouraged and on the run, seeking refuge in a cave. He was expecting God to speak to him in dramatic ways in a mighty wind, an earthquake, or a fire. But the Bible says that God wasn't in any of those things. Instead, God's voice came in a "still small voice" (1 Kings 19:12). Elijah had to quiet his mind and listen closely to hear God's direction.

In the same way, God is calling you to moments of silence so that He can speak directly to your heart.

Silence before God is not weakness; it is strength and when you sit quietly before God, you are demonstrating trust and acknowledging that your strength comes from Him, not from your own efforts.

Wisdom Capsules

1. "Insist of establishing a voice in the spirit realm that 1000 years from today it continues to echo in the spirit. There is something about your voice that brings your portion. It is the mind and the heart of God to constantly make you a living testimony and stronger force above the plots and plans of the enemy." - ADP

2. "There are those who believe that life getting you down is an opportunity for them to get at you. God knows about your enemies and He is greater than our enemies. He is working on revealing Himself and His glory, might, and power." - ADP

3. "Do not live your life thinking about enemies. Live your life thinking about God - He knows how to handle your enemies." - ADP

4. "The best way to live is in the presence and will of God." - ADP

5. "The smartest way to live is in the obedience of God." - ADP

6. "God is going to make things work for your good that all day and every day, you will have a shout. God will give you your shout!" - ADP

7. "A focused whisper is a loud voice. It is the power of a focused life. When whisper is focused, it becomes a sound voice. God is moving you from being a whisper to be loud until you become a voice." - ADP

8. "Every time your life is quiet; God is building momentum inside." - ADP

9. "There is a phase when God wants you to be quiet and there is a phase when He places a higher demand on your life, not to punish you but to polish you, because He is about to publish you. When your set time comes, you do not cool off on God - instead increase your efforts." - ADP

10. "There are things that have kept you in silence, in the cocoon, and darkness, but these things are about to come down. You must be determined to shout loud, and to stand loud, you have to shout." - ADP

11. "When God wants to give you a loud life, the first thing He does is reveal Himself to you." - ADP

12. "Nothing pleases God like a man or woman who positions themselves for God and who gives God the opportunity and the room to turn their mockery into glory." - ADP

13. "Anytime Satan wants to waste your life, he begins to negotiate your commitment and he tells you to take it easy." - ADP

14. "Anything you contend with an attack in the spirit realm becomes a mantle you carry in the earthly realm." - ADP

15. "Satan's assignment is to silence your glory. He successfully silences your glory by silencing your song. When you praise, God raises!" - ADP

16. "Every generation has a role to play in either preparing or destroying the next generation." - ADP

17. "A man can cry in the arms of a strong man, not in the arms of a weak man." - ADP

18. "Satan's great agenda is to make the human race useless and fail God to the point that he can laugh at God. God is also at work to ensure His chosen race prevails and brings Him the glory. Part of your assignment is to introduce God to your world." - ADP

19. "God is raising a generation of men/women/boys/girls that will stand loud and confident appreciating who they are until God makes them into what He wants them to be." - ADP

20. "Choice one: comfort, convenience, or commitment." - ADP

21. "When God is working on you, He forms you from the inside and gives you the capacity to be His container, so that by the time you begin to shout, you are firmly formed." - ADP

22. "Real corruption is when you put in effort and instead of being rewarded or awarded for your effort, you are being destroyed just for that effort." - ADP

23. "Many cancel their portion when they are face-to-face with their situation. If your heart is with God, He will keep you on the right path!" - ADP

24. "Excellence will disrupt your thinking. It will disrupt your friendships." - ADP

25. "In the largeness of God, you are not lost. In your stupid stupidity, He still cares." - ADP

26. "Humility will get you any kind of prosperity that stupidity cannot take from you." - ADP

27. "Many have missed what God had for them because when they were close to receiving that mantle they went off-course and self-got in the way. If you do not overcome self, there is no place for you in the Kingdom of God." - ADP

28. "There are moves you make and attitudes you develop that impress God. When you impress God, nothing can suppress your destiny." - ADP

29. "The man that stays consistent becomes the man that gets the attention of angels." - ADP

30. "Many people are blind spiritually, so they cannot see what is ahead. They are stumbling into the future - breaking ranks." - ADP

31. "When you take your eyes off of God, the feet that was meant to help you will end up being the feet that trips you." - ADP

32. "The enemy is a master at blocking and closing things. He likes to open that which will lead to hell and close that which will lead to glory." - ADP

33. "There is a healing hand, a prosperity hand, a vision hand, a power hand, a career hand, and a glory hand. Receive whatever you desire." - ADP

34. "How does the prophetic work? Sometimes and most times, it is your ability to discern and respond to the ridiculous that determines and opens up the miraculous for your destiny." - ADP

35. "You cannot deal with mighty evil spirits by being casual in your approach." - ADP36. "Shining forth is being able to produce results in such a way that proves that God is on your side and you are on God's side." - ADP

37. "Never mistake satanic attack for divine purging." - ADP

38. "Some people know and understand the timing but they miss the instruction. When you are in your set time, you hardly stand under pressure. The tendency to let go is the strongest when you are close to your set time." - ADP

39. "It is never the joy of God that you rise and go down. He wants you to keep rising." - ADP

40. "There is no investment you make in being wise that is ever a waste. Wisdom will always find its level!" - ADP

41. "It is wisdom to know that you need to be wise. It is impossible for anyone who cannot be corrected to be wise. When people fail to learn, Satan keeps winning." - ADP

42. "When you ignore the sign and jump into the covenant, you will miss it. When you ignore the covenant and jump into the sign, you will miss it. There has to be a combination of the sign and the covenant." - ADP

43. "Inspiration excites you. Instruction establishes you.

Excitement fluctuates. A combination of enthusiasm and instruction is what establishes a great destiny." - ADP

44. "You can tear something down in one day but it takes a lifetime to build it back up." - ADP

45. "You must build to know that whatever you are building withstands the wind, the rain, and the flood when it comes to test it. It must be rooted down else it crumbles down." - ADP

46. "Make it a point of duty to study how mighty people fall." - ADP

47. "Your life, your destiny, your future, and your dream is a building. The foundation may be ugly and rough, but a strong foundation holds an entire building up." - ADP

48. "The presence of rain is a blessing that proves what you are building. Whether you like it or not, it will rain and the rain will produce floods. If you do not build it strong, life will sweep it away." - ADP

49. "The only way to prove the authenticity of God is to put it in fire. A way to test the authenticity of humans is to give them fame." - ADP

50. "Every time a person settles within their heart that they are planted in Him and a spiritual lineage, God begins to breathe within them and their efforts. Every time you receive the revelation of the Holy One, you are enjoying God." - ADP

51. "As restless spirit comes when it notices that you are about to be elevated. Then everything about your life becomes unstable. Restlessness usually arrests a weak spirit." - ADP

52. "A seductive spirit will misinterpret instructions meant to take you to high places and will make you embrace failure. If you do not have strong wings, you cannot fly." - ADP

53. "Show me a person who does not have personal devotion and

I will show you a person who always falls for the seductress. In the place of true personal devotion, God talks to you." - ADP

54. "Activity is not what impresses the Lord - it is your ability to wise up because God can use a wise person more than He can use a foolish person." - ADP

55. "When the spirit of the desert catches up with a person, that person becomes a victim of it." - ADP

56. "Foolishness is the absence of wisdom. A foolish woman over time tears down her own house." - ADP

57. "Choices reveal wisdom or foolishness. Wisdom is reflected in your decisions." - ADP

58. "The key to being wise is to be undistracted." - ADP

59. "In order to be undistracted, you must have a focus worthy of your attention and focus. The proof of wisdom is by being focused." - ADP

CHAPTER EIGHT

CONQUERING DARKNESS

*Wisdom, Humility, and the
Call to Greatness*

D arkness, as described in Scripture, symbolizes sin, ignorance, and the forces of evil that seek to consume the light in you. To conquer this darkness, you must first recognize that the battle is spiritual, not physical and that your weapons are not of this world. Yes, they are not of this world because it is God who equips you with the necessary tools to overcome darkness, wisdom, humility, and the divine call to greatness. You should know that wisdom is your first and essential weapon. It is not human intelligence or cleverness, but godly wisdom that will give you clarity in the face of confusion. Proverbs 4:7 says "get wisdom" above all else. When facing darkness, whether in the form of temptation, discouragement, or opposition, wisdom will allow you to see beyond the immediate and recognize the larger spiritual battle at play. It gives you the insight to make choices that honor God, leading you into victory over every challenge.

Also wisdom without humility can lead to pride, and pride will lead to spiritual defeat. Jesus, the greatest example of humility, conquered the power of darkness not by force, but through submission to the will of the Father. Philippians 2:8 tells us that He humbled Himself unto death, even the death of the cross. To conquer darkness, you must learn to humble yourself under God's mighty hand, allowing Him to exalt you in His time.

Finally, the **call to greatness** is the final element of conquering darkness. You must realize that God has placed a unique calling on your life that is tied to His glory. You were created for more than mere existence; you were created to shine and that is why Matthew 5:16 says, "Let your light so shine before men, that they may see your good works and glorify your Father which is in heaven." Greatness in God's eyes is not about fame or recognition, but about walking in the purpose He has ordained for you. When you answer this call with boldness and faith, you become a light that dispels the darkness around you.

Wisdom Capsules

1. "A foolish person is a person without the right information." - ADP

2. "A foolish person is a person without the complete information." - ADP

3. "A foolish person is a person with complete information but refuses to take the right action (that is, a person who has information but lacks application)." - ADP

4. "A person who does not invest in finding the right focus and strengthening their focus in a way that makes their distractions evaporate." - ADP

5. "What makes a person wise and keeps them wise: you walk up to the street into a life with meaning when you choose to be wise." - ADP

6. "Being wise is impossible if there is no personal conviction

and persuasion. It is impossible to have personal conviction and persuasion if you do not have certain things you are focused on." - ADP

7. "If you focus on what is right, you will be wise, and as you are wise, you will grow and succeed to your advantage. When you have something important to focus on, those who do not have anything to focus on become easily distracted." - ADP

8. "Never underestimate the demands of destiny, especially as you make progress." - ADP

9. "Set your mind and heart right because the Spirit of the Lord is about to use you." - ADP

10. "Choose the path of being wise. Pay the price of wisdom! Do not go through life without knowing what to do with life. Look up to Jesus and look to Him to help you!" - ADP

11. "You are being sent out as sheep in the midst of wolves. The only way you can make it is to be as wise as a serpent and as harmless as a dove!" - ADP

12. "If you lack the wiseness of serpents, you will become food to wolves." - ADP

13. "God cannot use foolish people." - ADP

14. "God wants to extinct darkness! Everything dark repels God. God hates anything and everything dark." - ADP

15. "One of the purposes of man is to ensure that darkness ceases to exist." - ADP

16. "Darkness exists in the realm of man only, not in the realm of God!" - ADP

17. "God has already ordained certain laws into the universe. Any and everything that is impure fades. The universe has purity in it. The universe has been created to work and respond

to the pure. This is one thing that is a headache to Satan." - ADP

18. "A pure heart will constantly win. It will interpret things the right way." - ADP

19. "Everything on earth has its purpose!" - ADP

20. "The devil knows how powerful God's truth is, so the only way he can work against God in any way is to get man to pervert the truth of God. Getting man to pervert the truth of God makes man weak and makes man unable to divert his schemes." - ADP

21. "God's truth ordained that every time man works with God and responds to God the right way, the universe bows to the man." - ADP

22. "God may not always make you the head of an assignment, but He makes you the help of the assignment. No head ever truly succeeds without help." - ADP

23. "The worst warfare that man has ever faced is the warfare where helpers become hurters. Warfare hardly gets to the head because the head has enough light and resistance." - ADP

24. "You can never win with God if you ignore the fact that Satan is constantly working closer to see how to make you irrelevant and inconsequential." - ADP

25. "Darkness is pain." - ADP

26. "Every one of us has a role to play in defeating darkness, and until you respond to greatness, you will never understand your role in defeating darkness." - ADP

27. "Only a pure heart survives and thrives through the onslaught of darkness." - ADP

28. "Most times, you do not value the place of grace and mercy until you are kicked outside to the place of toiling." - ADP

29. "If you do not learn how to leave Goliath headless, you will be shocked how Goliath will revive himself to bring you down to the place he wants you to be." - ADP

30. "God has an idea—that darkness in all of its forms and shapes must be defeated. Darkness that is not recognized, arrested, and defeated becomes darkness that destroys greatness." - ADP

31. "The entire fight of the human race is the Genesis 1:4 fight. Darkness is still a part of everything we do." - ADP

32. "When you ignore the blessings of a father, you will constantly fail and struggle." - ADP

33. "It is possible for you to win at all times. The more you win, the more hell hates you, but who cares! Our assignment is to confront and defeat hell." - ADP

34. "Lack of humility will make you transfer responsibilities. The sign of a prideful person is the refusal to accept responsibility for their wrong." - ADP

35. "There is nothing as sweet as owning up to your foolishness." - ADP

36. "Your superpower is that you must work with God in spirit and in truth. The super life is the life God has ordained for you." - ADP

37. "No one can pass the test to and for greatness for you but you." - ADP

38. "The call to greatness is a powerful call to defeat darkness. Every time God calls good things to your life, evil things come along." - ADP

39. "The call to greatness is the call for all. Anyone who thinks greatness is not important will take the backseat of life." - ADP

40. "The call to stand with God and represent God on the earth.

To represent the power, wisdom, and grace of God on earth." - ADP

41. "The call to drive out, defeat darkness, and separate darkness from your soul and the church." - ADP

42. "The worst nightmare you can face is to fight the one who is ordained to bring you out of warfare." - ADP

43. "Man will need the light of God to defeat darkness. Darkness will never be man's friend." - ADP

44. "Humility. There are very few people that respond to God in humility. God will never invest true light in a proud soul. The spirit of pride sponsors sorrow. It takes a lot of humility to walk with God." - ADP

45. "Man's responsibility is to collaborate with God and defeat darkness. Darkness exists in the realm of man, and based on God's law that governs the universe, God's creation has to be the one to defeat darkness, not God." - ADP

46. "The garden was a place of concentrated presence of God. Light refers to God's concentrated presence. The more Adam stayed in the garden, the more he had concentrated power over the earth." - ADP

47. "By reason of staying in the presence of God, Moses carried a glory that the people could not look in his face." - ADP

48. "It may look cheap avoiding light that comes from God's presence, but in the long run, you will pay dearly for it. The weakness of man is never a threat to God. The hatred for God's presence is what God hates in man." - ADP

49. "Everyone conquered by darkness will never partake of God's greatness. You are called to defeat darkness." - ADP

50. "The moment you begin to sense victory, your winning ticket is high humility. It is humility that begins to interpret things to

you. The power of unity and purity!" - ADP

51. "The spirit of affliction thrives on an individual's ability to use light to keep affliction away. Satan is so scared of your stability that he will always create battles a second time to make it a pattern. Patterns are stronger than demons." - ADP

52. "Do not let the darkness of the earth defeat you. Do not stay in the place where darkness has more power than you. Humility is key in staying in God's presence. A humble heart is an easy workshop for God." - ADP

53. "Invite the searching light of God into your heart and your spirit, after which God will give you instructions." - ADP

54. "The word of God is the light within you. Carriers of light become torturers of darkness. The greatest key to dominion is illumination - light!" - ADP

55. "One of the gifts of a father is depth, insight, and revelation." - ADP

56. "When God made the earth (His first creation), He rented it. But when He made man, He gifted the earth to man and He gave the man the title deed. He never gave it to demons." - ADP

57. "I wonder what you have been losing because Satan has been taking." - ADP

58. "God created man so that man can cooperate with Him and defeat darkness because darkness was not part of the original plan." - ADP

59. "God values people, but many are not trustworthy. God is counting on you to change the world you live in today. He knows that with your presence, something will get better." - ADP60. "God is expecting you to lead in your generation. Through your leadership, people will find and follow God. Everyone has the ability to lead. Every follower must think like a leader.

Discipleship never succeeds until the disciple begins to think of mastery." - ADP

61. "The best that God gives to man is based on their ability to understand their purpose and mandate. Anyone who understands the concept of protection and preservation will always enjoy the best of God. You must accept responsibility to protect anything that you are a part of." - ADP

62. "Blessing is the ability to transfer goodwill to someone under you." - ADP

63. "Spiritual blessing is the impartation of goodness, glory, and spirit that assists people to make them stars in life." - ADP

64. "When God is calling your warfare, do not chase fun-fare or sympathy." - ADP

65. "So long as night exists in a life, there is room for sorrow." - ADP

66. "Respect a great person. A great person is one who masters the art of conquering their weakness just to help others become great and better." - ADP

67. "Protect anyone that is strong in your life. Protect strong people in your life." - ADP

68. "Teach your children how to protect greatness." - ADP

69. "The blessing of a father removes reproach from lives and corrects the future before error takes place." – ADP

CHAPTER NINE

THE PATH TO GREATNESS & EXCEPTIONAL LIVING

"Wisdom, Vision, and Divine Principles"

Greatness in life is not defined by wealth, fame, or worldly success, but by living according to God's purpose. To achieve this, you need divine wisdom, a clear vision, and a commitment to God's principles. Wisdom, as Proverbs reminds us, is the foundation of a godly life. It helps you make choices that align with God's will and guides you through the challenges you face. Wisdom keeps you on the path of righteousness, avoiding distractions that lead to failure.

Vision gives you clarity about your purpose because when you live with vision, you see beyond the present and focus on the future that God has prepared for you. Without vision, you will wander aimlessly, but with it, you are driven by God's purpose, confident that He is directing your steps.

To walk the path of greatness, seek God's wisdom, embrace His vision, and live by His principles. In doing so, you will live a life of purpose, peace, and divine favor.

Greatness Talks About:

1. Greatness talks about a remarkable life.

2. Greatness talks about an exceptional life.

3. Greatness talks about a life that is able to bring ashes together and turn it into beauty.

4. Ability to take lead and keep leading.

5. Legacy.

6. Making an impact.

7. Selflessly serving your generation.

8. Proper use of your talent, ability, and skills to do good things and make the world a better place.

9. The ability to have a clear vision.

10. Exceptional achievement.

Keys Is To Greatness:

1. Humility.

2. Accountability.

3. You making your mind to embrace the vision of God.

4. Being a problem solver.

5. Your willingness to be properly trained to achieve what God has for you.

Know This

1. "It is never God's will for you to be defeated, stagnated, or be at a low place in life." - ADP

2. "You cannot change the world and make a difference by

protesting. You change the world and make a difference by projecting." - ADP

3. "Mountains are elevated platforms. It is wrong for you to start your world in the valley and end up in the valley." - ADP

4. "There are things God ordained for us, expects for us, and expects from us. God expects you to be successful and outstanding, but Satan does everything to make you God's nightmare." - ADP

5. "If you do not follow God well, Satan will create monsters in your life. Midgets will become monsters—pebbles will become mountains—dwarfs and grasshoppers will become giants. But if you have God, the reverse happens" - ADP

6. Nobody ever invests their time growing up with God and then ends up losers in life. - ADP

7. "You are hurting yourself and your destiny when you trust in men and your career more than you trust in God." - ADP

8. "A man/woman who does not believe or trust in God becomes an easy target for evil spirits." - ADP

9. "If you build your life around God, it doesn't matter who is trying to take you down, God will ensure that they go down!" - ADP

10. "Shining forth is an agenda, and until you shine, the agenda is lame! You cannot shine forth by talking alone. You shine forth by shining forth."

To Shine Forth Means:

1. To stand up in life.

2. To stand tall in life.

3. To stand out in life.

Take Note

1. "Your life should have a mark of difference—a mark of uniqueness. There should be a mark on your life that tells the world that you are special." - ADP

2. "This is God's expectation—that your life stands up, stands out, and stands tall." - ADP

3."Jumping from heights naturally takes you down, except you are equipped with a certain device that suspends the law of gravity. If you do not pay attention to the guiding principles of God, no matter how high you rise, you will go down. That's a fact!" - ADP

4. "Because you are special, God has giv en you the guiding principles. - Deuteronomy 26:18-19 Msg Principles that seem too tall to attain are meant for the protection of high things. Do not get mad at these principles." - ADP

5. "People died from Mount Everest not because the mountain threw them down, but they realized that the higher they climbed, the thinner the air was and the violence of the wind. Weak lungs lose the ability to breathe well.

6. "It is the will of God that you and I rise to the top!" - ADP

7. "God wants you to set records. Satan likes it when you settle down in mediocrity." - ADP

8. "In order to shine forth, you have to be a trailblazer—a record breaker—a pathfinder—an individual who intentionally makes sense of their lives. Shine forth to shine forth refers to you learning and mastering some practical steps to take in order to fulfill God's shining forth mandate for your life to become an experience. To shine forth to shine forth, there is a deposit that is needed to be seen in you for your face to shine." – ADP

9. "What is the point of going through the process of being a

butterfly never to make it out of the cocoon?" - ADP

10. "When you become diligent in seeking what it takes to represent God on earth, you will be so shocked how fast God will lift and protect you. There should be such an ability of God within every child of God that will make men look at you with a sense of awe, regard, reverence, and dignity." - ADP

11. "Nothing brings greatness like a focused life!" - ADP

12 "If you must shine forth to shine forth, there are certain practical things that must be at work in your life." - ADP

13. "Disgrace is the inability to be an achiever. It is for you to be rejected instead of being celebrated, for life to give you a thumbs-down instead of a thumbs-up."

14. "It is never God's will for you to be humiliated. If you walk with God, the things that look like reproach are the very things that God will use to lift you up." - ADP

What Makes People Wise?

1. "If you ignore instructions, you will be a fool. The promotion of fools is failure/shame." - ADP

2 "In order to shine forth, the wiser you become, the shinier you shine. If you do not grow wiser, what looks like shine diminishes and begins to dim. Whatever stops growing starts dying and decaying." - ADP

3. "To wise up is to gain wisdom or common sense." - ADP

What It Means To Be Wise:

1. To have wisdom.

2. To have understanding of life and how it works.

3. To have and use discretion.

4. To have and use discernment.

5. To have and use common sense.

6. To have and use uncommon sense.

7. To learn, understand, and apply basic and major/fundamental principles that govern life...

8. To live a progressive and prosperous life that is inspiring and worthy of emulation...

CHAPTER TEN

SHINE FORTH

*Keys To Unlocking Greatness
And Overcoming Challenges*

You are called to shine as a beacon of hope and truth; Jesus declared that you are the world's light, a city set on a hill that cannot be hidden. This great truth should remind you of the incredible potential God has placed within you. Your light is not just for your benefit; it is meant to illuminate the darkness around you, guiding others to the hope and love found in Christ. Your light can break through the darkness in today's world, filled with challenges, confusion, and despair.

Wisdom Capsules

1. "To rise, you have to have a dream." - ADP

2. "Life works for dreamers. If you do not have a dream, your life is doomed! Stop living for survival—start thriving." - ADP

3. "Never allow people's opinion decide your dominion." - ADP

4. "Whenever you waste a miracle, you live with obstacles. Judge wisely before you make certain decisions." - ADP

5. "If you do not have and use discretion, you are not wise and

cannot shine forth. You will hurt and ruin people, and God will not promote you." - ADP

6. "The broken becomes a master at mending." - ADP

7. "You must discern people, atmospheres, favors, irritations, rejection, jobs, careers. You must interpret and discern." - ADP

8. "Wise up to shine forth." - ADP

9. "Do not keep your options open—keep your heart focused!" - ADP

10. "Do not steal from God to rise to the top." - ADP

11. "Give to God so that God will give you that which you cannot give to yourself." - ADP

12. "The place of devotion helps you interpret life's battles." - ADP

13. "It is possible to have opportunities and end as a destitute." - ADP - Psalm 49:20 TPT

14. "The greater people you have around you, the easier it is for you to establish greatness within and around you." - ADP

15. "It is not your career that makes you prosperous; it is the one who carries you that makes you prosperous." - ADP

16. "When it comes to visitations and encounters, individuals determine their portion." - ADP

17. "The devil's goal is to mess and destroy you." - ADP

18. "Everybody has a mouth until it is time to pay the price. Talk is cheap." - ADP

19. "Devotion is the place of interpretation." - ADP

20. "Only if you will allow God to cultivate your heart and put in the dedication and focus needed." - ADP

21. "Your devotion determines your destiny devotion." - ADP

22. "Great people want to see hunger." - ADP

23. "Nothing works until you are willing to work it." - ADP

24. "Life will never waste its treasure investing in someone who will never appreciate the investment of life in him/her." - ADP

25. "Great people look for those who can keep treasures and handle precious things." - ADP

26. "When people cannot handle precious things, they criticize those who produce precious things!" - ADP

27. "Careless living is the cheapest way to live until you live a little longer and find out that the more useless way to live is a careless life." - ADP

28. "Careless people never keep treasures." - ADP

29. "Great people look for loyalty." - ADP - Luke 9:23 TPT

30. "You know who is loyal by finding out who is present when you need strength." - ADP

31. "Make yourself loyal, and greatness will draw you to great people." - ADP

32. "Great people look for zero toxicity." - ADP

33. "Make life so easy that you can easily handle difficult things." - ADP

34. "Do not be a rebel." - ADP

35. "Make yourself less toxic. Great people will keep you in their presence for a long time." - ADP

36. "Greatness comes with a lot of hard work, and great people depend on those who have staying power." - ADP

37. "No greatness comes until people have opposed you. Then the great person who is supposed to give you your greatness becomes the last hurdle you have to deal with." - ADP

38. "When great people test you with tolerance and endurance, do not fail the test." - ADP

39. "Most people miss greatness when they get to a place of greatness, and there is high demand." - ADP

40. "Pressure will reveal toxicity." - ADP

41. "Trust God to check areas of your life where you might be toxic." - ADP

42. "Racism and sexism are useless in the presence of excellence." - ADP

43. "The one that is consistent is the one with the most chance of being loyal." - ADP

44. "It is always easier to walk alone than to drag a dead body." - ADP

45. "A person who you have always to drag can slow you down." - ADP

46. "You must be willing to be patient with people's weaknesses to lead them to greatness." - ADP

47. "Up your personal devotion life." - ADP

48. "Your devotion brings an interpretation of your life and journey." - ADP

49. "Up your devotion game. Read the Bible, talk to God, hear from God." - ADP

50. "Up your intercession life." - ADP

51. "One of the best gifts you can give to yourself now is to catch

the spirit of prayer." - ADP

52. "Intercession is different from devotion." - ADP

53. "Devotion is the place where you grow with God and allow God to speak to you—intercession is the process of rearranging things in the spirit realm through the process of concentrated and consistent prayer." - ADP

54. "Intercession births interception." - ADP

55. "Intercession helps you to accomplish interception—intercepting the arrows, bullies, and wicked things of the enemy and all that Satan is doing." - ADP

56. "The more missiles you intercept, the more you waste the arrows of the enemy." - ADP

57. "Interception is interference—you are interfering with the enemy's affair." - ADP

58. "Never allow a battle to come to you before you react." - ADP

59. "God gives strength to those that take the battle to the gate." - ADP

60. "You become the disturbance of the programs of the enemy." - ADP

61. "Every time you interfere with Satan's affairs, you irritate hell." - ADP

62. "Intercession gives you the power to interfere with Satan's affairs regarding your life and that of your loved ones." - ADP

63. "Intercession is one of the most powerful ways to receive power and spiritual authority in a discounted way." - ADP

64. "Intercession brings you promotion and makes you an authority in the city." - ADP - Daniel 10:12-13

65. "You master intercession by mastering night vigils." - ADP

66. "Up your adoration life." - ADP

67. "Combine any and everything with praise and gratitude." - ADP

68. "Up your pursuit of excellence." - ADP

69. "Up your desire for excellence." - ADP

70. "Never want to be just a regular person." - ADP

71. "Make up your mind to be an extraordinary person whose life will change things and bring people to God." - ADP

72. "Make up your mind to be excellent in your disposition." - ADP

73. "Whatever it will require for you to be an evangelist, go get wood." - ADP

74. "Study how to grow church, how to win people, how to bring people to God's house." - ADP

75. "Study how to be a contributor, how not to be a liability, how not to bring regret to the body of God, how never to be the scapegoat." - ADP

76. "Decide to be the one that brings wood to build the house of God." - ADP - Proverbs 8:1-11 Msg

77. "There are certain things that should be your personal affairs. Guard them with discretion." - ADP

78. "Your calling is unique." - ADP

79. "You should not tell everybody about things God has called you to do." - ADP

80. "Do not tell everybody." - ADP

81. "Take time to guard your prayer life—evil imagination always births affliction." - ADP - Proverbs 8:1-11 MSG

82. "Have an open mind and heart towards truth." - ADP

83. "Be able to look at life as taking pictures without filters." - ADP

84. "Do not use filters to judge your growth." - ADP

85. "Look at the mirror of life without filters." - ADP

86. "I am your blesser, not your wrestler." - ADP - Apostle Dr. David Philemon

87. "The most stupid thing to do is to wrestle with God." - ADP

88. "No one ever wrestles with God. You submit to God and you resist the devil—and the devil will have to flee from you." - ADP

89. "When you find yourself fighting all the time, it is due to the pride, toxicity, and wickedness of your heart." - ADP

90. "God will take me to where destiny is the best." - ADP - Proverbs 8:1-11 Msg

91. "Nobody succeeds without discipline." - ADP

92. "Practice self-control and accept responsibility." - ADP

93. "Walk through life with meaning." - ADP

94. "There are people that will envy you." - ADP

CHAPTER ELEVEN

LIVING WITH PURPOSE

"The Power Of Alignment, Devotion, And Kingdom Responsibility"

L iving with purpose is a lifestyle that requires intentional alignment with God's will, heartfelt devotion, and a clear understanding of your responsibilities in His Kingdom. God desires that you not only know your purpose but actively pursue it, reflecting His love and light in everything you do. You should know that alignment is key to living purposefully.

Just as a car needs to be aligned for optimal performance, your life must be aligned with God's truth. This means examining your priorities and desires and ensuring they are in line with His Word. When your heart is aligned with God, you'll find clarity in your decisions and direction in your path.

Successes To Have (In Order)

1. Spiritual Success

2. Mental Success

3. Physical Success

4. Health Success

Note:

1. "No one ever wastes his life and time waiting upon God. He knows your needs, fears, and battles." - ADP

2. "Only those with open minds understand." - ADP

3. "It is impossible to be insane when you embrace the wisdom of God." - ADP

4. "You will never find God's wisdom if you do not look for it. Without it, insanity becomes the portion of those who are pressing to achieve success." - ADP

5. "When you earn the killing of Goliath, the throne of the lion is no longer a threat to you. But you must manage that throne with wisdom, dignity, kindness, and niceness." - ADP

Declare This: "My brain works with excellence!"

6. "You will never succeed until you understand that what you are doing is significant." - ADP

7. "You are God's distribution center." - ADP

8. "Your life is significant! You are important, and your contribution matters!" -ADP

9. "A mountain refers to stability, solidity, protection." - ADP

10. "Satan will rather give you pebbles than allow you to have mountains." - ADP

11. "If your interest and hunger is flat, you will never get the best of God. It is called indifference." - ADP

12. "Just because there is an agenda does not mean that every day is the calendar. It is your personal responsibility to push in!" - ADP

13. "It is spirit that makes people fail and succeed." - ADP

14. "Anytime you appreciate and celebrate any help from God, you give God the license to solidify your life." - ADP

15. "Every time you respect what God respects, you should expect a major release and reward from God." - ADP

16. "Nothing in this life happens by mistake—good or bad." - ADP

17. "As far as God is concerned, we are in the days of receiving all!" - ADP

18. "It is spirits that lift men up and it is spirits that bring men down." - ADP

19. "Satan attacks your mind and limits you to you." - ADP

20. "The moment you get God's attention; you enjoy His invitation." - ADP

21. "Many times, most people do everything possible to get the attention of God and the moment that they get God's attention, they destroy what cost them years to get because they become so careless in their pursuits." -ADP

22. "What will happen to you if you know that in the next three months you will be a multi-millionaire? How will you respond to God's invitation today?" - ADP

23. "Many believers talk about what God will do and never experience what God has done." - ADP

24. "God gives you an appetizer just to wet your appetite. Yet, an appetizer is not as delicious as the main course. If you get full off of appetizers, you will miss the main course." - ADP

25. "Do not ever allow the king (the appetizer) to rob you of the reason why you came into the kingdom." - ADP

26. "If you fail to study why you are not experiencing the things God has in store for you, you will miss what God has for you." - ADP

27. "Most times, people glorify what they met and ignore what they miss." - ADP

28. "Do not let the acquisition of properties be the reason why you miss the whole real estate." -ADP

29. "When a prophet senses genuine hunger, he releases a prophetic destiny." - ADP

30. "There is nothing God hates like being an alternative in your life." - ADP

31. "When you run away from kingdom responsibility, you miss the approval and commendation from the Almighty God." - ADP

32. "Recognize that God is in a hurry to give you everything. All things are ready, but all men and women are not ready." - ADP

33. "Killing Goliath was Saul's responsibility, but killing Goliath was David's opportunity. Transfer of responsibility is the transfer of crown. Most times, people transfer their responsibility to people who are looking for opportunity." -ADP

34. "God is looking for heart, not height." - ADP

God is looking for:

1. A heart that will not make excuses. - Luke 14:20-21 TPT

2. A heart that understands a call to distribution.

3. A heart that understands that when the anointing comes, and you are given unction, it is for distribution.

4. A heart that understands that there are destinies that need to be unlocked.

5. A heart that accepts kingdom responsibility.

6. A heart that deletes spiritual irresponsibility.

7. A heart that wants things to happen God's way, not your way.

8. A heart that decides to be fully raised by God.

9. A heart that wants all that God has for you and for your generation—becoming a distribution center.

Note:

1. "God likes to consolidate and concentrate His greatness, oil, unction, power, and glory in an individual. Not everyone has the discipline, commitment, and determination to fit into His plan." - ADP

2. "Do not settle for less. Go for everything, including the things you do not need." - ADP

3. "Common sense is good, but common sense will not give you superior destiny." - ADP

4. "It is your response that determines your portion." - ADP

5. "When your love for God begins to dwindle, the work of God begins to slow down." - ADP

6. "What permits the work of God to continue in our lives is the burning love of God." - ADP

7. "Nothing you have even been through should be wasted. Nothing that you are going through should be wasted.

God hates wasting the details of our life." - ADP

8. "It is an error for the pain you have been through in life to not add something to where you are going to in life." - Romans 8:28 Tpt

9. "If you refuse to submit an aspect of your life to God, it becomes difficult for Him to weave that aspect into your destiny. Most times, the very detail we think we need to keep away from God is the very detail that God wants to weave into our purpose." - ADP

10. "Prophets are God's braiders. When God wants to weave your life together, He arranges a prophet and a prophetic meeting." - ADP

11. "Your hunger is the currency needed to purchase your prophecy." - ADP

12. "Your prophecy is the currency needed to fulfill your future." - ADP

13. "The things that appear useless become useful in the atmosphere of the prophetic." - 1 Samuel 8:18-19 Tlb

14. "Everyone might have been saying there is no help for me in God, but 'now' the saying is different." - Psalm 3:2-3, 6 Amp/Msg

15. "One of the evidences when a man is lifted up is that God gives him a new song." – ADP

Declare This: "I too will testify (give witness) of the greatness of my God. 'I too.'" - Psalms 135:5 Msg

Note:

1. "To be a witness, you are to have some kind of evidence." - ADP

2. "A witness is one who saw something." - ADP

3. "God did not send me here to look for money. He sent me here as an ambassador." - ADP

4. "If you try to outsmart God, you will fail. It is foolishness to try to outsmart God." - ADP

5. "There is no end to life's problems—submit your life to God and submit your life to the path He has set. Serving God does not pay when you serve Him wrong." - ADP

6. "There is nothing God says that God cannot or will not do if man stays with God." - ADP

7. "All the things you are chasing are shadows and vanity. Chase God!" - ADP

8. "No one ever abandons himself in God's care and ends up a misfit or a loser. Stop chasing shadows!" - ADP

9. "It is the will of God for everything to go your way so long as that which is going your way does not get into your head." - ADP

10. "You cannot blackmail God. The best thing to do is to align with Him." - ADP

11. "You either fall in or you fall out. Your heart must submit and align." - ADP

12. "The worst thing you can do is to give God a toxic heart and expect Him to use that kind of toxic heart on the earth." - ADP

13. "If God is taking His time to work on your heart now, it is because He knows that your mindset cannot accommodate the

CHAPTER TWELVE

POWER KEYS
TO RISING AND
STAYING UP

Embracing Responsibility,
Obedience, and Purpose"

T aking responsibility for your life is crucial to personal growth and spiritual maturity. You should know that God has given you free will, and with that comes the responsibility to make choices that shape your life. In Galatians 6:5, we are reminded that "every man shall bear his burden." This shows the importance of owning your actions and decisions because they will directly impact your life and the lives of those around you. When you take responsibility, you empower yourself to create change. Instead of blaming circumstances or others for your situation, you acknowledge that you can influence your outcomes.

This shift in mindset is liberating. It will allow you to recognize that you are not a victim of your circumstances but rather an active participant in your life's outcomes.

Power keys to rising and staying up!

1. "The essence of going through is not to go through but to get through." - ADP

2. "God does not give a great future if you do not manage the little test." - ADP

3. "A lift refers to a rise, a change of position, and a change of status." - ADP

4. "Hard work is not what makes great men. Favored work is what makes great men." - ADP

5. "Word is not work until instruction is received. Any promise that comes to you without an instruction to navigate is not a complete word or revelation. Any complete revelation that comes from God is the one that tells you your own path." - ADP

6. "Your own path is not as convenient but as responded. It is when the word marries the name that the word responds to fame." - ADP

7. "Your knowledge has become your demise. Take that knowledge and turn it to revelation." - ADP

8. "Do not settle for the status quo. There is more to life than you have seen!" - ADP

9. "There are natural ways to rise and there are supernatural ways to rise." - ADP

10. "The supernatural lift is when a man or woman positions themselves in a way that God finds something within you that says you are ready for God and God cuts all protocol to become your coach." - ADP

11. "Why does God work in the hearts of people? So that He can give them a place on the Earth." - ADP

12. "God wants you to rise because He gets the chance to prove to the world how good, merciful, and kind He is." - ADP

13. "Being lifted refers to being able to connect with your purpose in a passionate and strong way that every atmosphere you influence reveals the purpose God called you to accomplish." - ADP

14. "Being lifted refers to being a success story and a shining star in either the field you have chosen in the guidance of God for you." - ADP

15. "Being lifted refers to your ability to connect with the God of Heaven to handle complications, adversities, contradictions and turn it all into ingredients and materials that make you a shining star." - ADP

16. "So people get inspired by your life by the fact that you have been able to navigate through the complication of life and God gets the glory." - ADP

17. "Being lifted refers to moving from a mere man to a great leader." - ADP

18. "Mere shepherds can become great leaders if they allow God to lift them." - ADP

19. "The secret of David's rise was his ability to get the attention of God through his devotion, dedication, and consecration. His heartbeat matched God's heartbeat. God did not find him by mistake. He lived the life that caught God's attention." - ADP

20. "Taking God out of the equation of life is your personal sign-up for frustration." - ADP

21. "Greatness is not for small minds!" - ADP

David had a passion to protect assets!

22. "Passion to protect greatness and anything God is doing is a

requirement." - ADP

23. "Every life must be centered around God's Kingdom. Any life centered around God's Kingdom never sinks." - ADP

24. "Most people miss supernatural liftings because they do not know how to secure God's presence or keep God with them. The presence of God is the lifter of men. His absence leads to the collapse of those who rose." - ADP

25. "When God is chasing you, it is for your own good. When God is working hard on changing you from the inside, it is because He wants to remove what is taking you away from Him – the inconsistencies, pride, etc." - ADP

26. "Most times, the presence of enemies always leads to the delay and hindrance of your progress. So God handles them by destroying them." - ADP

27. "Prophecy reveals God's expectation." - ADP

28. "You have to be on the move in the right direction. That which you are looking for has an address." - ADP

29. "My number one care is God and His people." - ADP

30. "Whatever threatens your destiny must be silenced by you. It is an instruction." - ADP

31. "God is in a hurry to raise examples – personal billboards. God wants to advertise Himself in a very unique way." - ADP

32. "The ugliness of your situation is an opportunity for God to reveal the beauty of God." - ADP

33. "The Lord framed the universe for transactions, profitability, and business. For example, He framed the ground to always release results to whoever blesses it with a seed." - ADP

34. "The Lord framed the universe for transactions, profitability,

and business. The key is marketing!" - ADP

35. "God wants to dress you with success, glory, and wealth so that He can advertise you." - ADP

36. "Life is a journey. This journey is an adventure. God is adventurous." - ADP

37. "The feet of man is part of the major forces that gives man his place on Earth." - ADP

38. "God gave you feelings. Not feelings to destroy you but feelings to bring you closer to Him and feelings to enjoy your progress and achievement. This is one of the major purposes of emotions. If you follow all your feelings, you will harm yourself." - ADP

39. "Satan will keep you away from walking with God because no one walks with God and misses good." - ADP

40. "There is something about God's power that when He walks in a place, He births prosperity, protection, and victory." - ADP

41. "God is removing the spirit of up and down from your feet." - ADP

42. "Your feet are a tool for the journey, and on this journey, you do not win by walking but by taking." - ADP

43. "Your feet, much more than tools for strolling, are weapons of possession. If you step your foot on it, it is yours." - ADP

44. "Your tomorrow should never be worse than your yesterday. Your today should never be better than your tomorrow. Your tomorrow should always be better than your today." - ADP

45. "Your feelings are the worst things to depend on when it comes to making decisions, fulfilling your calling, and making a life." - ADP

46. "Delayed obedience is disobedience. The more you delay obedience, the more you have a reason to disobey." - ADP

47. "Preeminence refers to the honor, dignity, and glory meant for you." - ADP

48. "Your destiny will never be yours until your obedience is complete. God will allow you to go back to the place where you missed your destiny through disobedience, and you obey Him again." - ADP

49. "Our acts of disobedience and rebellion to God is our indirect way of telling Him 'I am higher than you, wiser than you, or I want to be bigger than you.' Before God can take you higher, He has to stripe you of anything that looks like height." - ADP

50. "The things that God wants to do in your life requires that you pay a higher price. Never run away from burning fire to smoking wood." - ADP

51. "It is never God's intent that His will for you when revealed chase you away from Him. Ask for the grace to do the things that you do not know how to do naturally." - ADP

52. "You can run away from evil but never run away from responsibility, greatness, or destiny. You will never conquer what you are unwilling to confront. Do not run away from what will make you wealthy. Face it and find out how to fix it." - ADP

53. "A wandering feet:

   1. Causes your feet to walk into traps without knowing.

   2. Causes your feet to go everywhere but nowhere.

   3. Causes your feet to lead you to your failure and destruction."
- ADP

54. "A treated feet with remaining foolish emotions will stop you from entering the promised land." - ADP

55. "Men excel by secrets revealed. The secret of great men is in their story." - ADP

56. "Do whatever I can to secure the presence of God through living for God, loving God with all my heart, mind, soul, and entire life; and living a life of obedience to God's instruction." - ADP

57. "Living for God will put you in a place where God will constantly sanctify you. Any man or woman who lives for God constantly gets the attention of God." - ADP

58. "When you are generous to others in the area of kindness and mercy, God will ensure His presence stays with you." - ADP

59. "Always be happy when God wants to add something beautiful to someone even if you do not like them – look out for their welfare. Be generous towards the Kingdom of God." - ADP

60. "Fight the battles of God. Go out and fight God's battles – never allow yourself to ignore the battles of God. Whatever will make God's Kingdom stand out honorable above reproach should become your life's mandate." - ADP

CHAPTER THIRTEEN

POWER KEYS TO RISING, STAYING UP AND SHINING FORTH

"Knowledge and Divine Guidance"

In a world overflowing with information, the power of knowledge and divine guidance is paramount. Knowledge itself is not just about accumulating facts; it's about understanding God's truth and applying it to your life. Proverbs 2:6 reminds us that the Lord is the source of true wisdom, knowledge, and understanding. When you seek His guidance, you align yourself with His perfect plan for your life.

Know this: Knowledge empowers you to make informed decisions and navigate the complexities of life, but without divine guidance, that knowledge will lead you astray. It is essential to seek God's wisdom first and foremost. As you immerse yourself in His Word, He will reveal insights that surpass human understanding. Through prayer and meditation on Scripture, you can discern His voice, allowing His Spirit to lead you in every situation.

As you embrace the power of knowledge and divine guidance, remember that they work together harmoniously. Knowledge without guidance can confuse, while guidance without knowledge can lead to missteps. When you allow God's wisdom to shape your understanding, you will walk confidently in the path He has set for you.

Wisdom Capsules

1. "Every time you slow down or stop in your progress in the work of God, you stop many things." - ADP

2. "Do not slow down or cool off. You have to continue in the ways of God - pressing, fighting, and walking with God every single day." - ADP

3. "One of the best gifts God can give to you is the gift of knowing where God is taking you." - ADP

4. "You can put in so much labor, but it ends in weariness if you do not know how to go into the city." - ADP

5. "A fool does not know what to do or one who knows what to do but does not like to do it - one who does not know how to apply knowledge." - ADP

6. "Working smart is better than working hard. That you work hard is what makes you prosper." - ADP

7. "Working in the right direction is what brings great distinction." - ADP

8. "The lack of knowledge means a life that is not exposed to the right information." - ADP

9. "Knowledge is information. To be informed is almost to be transformed." - ADP

10. "It takes information to experience transformation - it takes information to escape deformation." - ADP

11. "What you do not know is greater than you." - ADP

12. "What you do not know can kill you." - ADP

13. "What you do not know can cost you your life, opportunities, privileges, and honor - it takes information to defeat frustration." - ADP

14. "The lack of knowledge means living a life where you have limited information." - ADP

15. "Where there is no knowledge, there is always failure." - ADP

16. "Until you know it, you cannot glow and flow in it." - ADP

17. "The word of God works hand in hand with the name of God. It is the promises of his word that authenticates the potency of his name." - ADP

18. "The lack of knowledge means perverted information - upside down information." - ADP

19. "The lack of knowledge means the absence of the revealed will of God with regards to the purpose (agenda), timing (calendar), process (principles), and person (the set man)." - ADP

20. "The lack of knowledge means the inability to put to use what is known to straighten the path that leads to where you are going." - ADP

21. "Most people know what to do, but they hate doing what they know." - ADP

22. "It is impossible for the path to the top to be easy unless you know where you are going." - ADP

23. "When you know where you are going to, you have to settle why you are going there." - ADP

24. "Intelligence is not enough to take you to the top. Applied intelligence is what takes you to the top." - ADP

25. "If you know what to do but lack the ability to take you where you need to go, you will stay where you are." - ADP

26. "Whenever God wants to help you truly, he doesn't just show you where you are going to, he shows you how to get to where you are going to." - ADP

27. "It is never God's intent for you to be lost and confused or for you to spend forever in an attempt for you to get to a certain destination." - ADP

28. "Most people get tired simply because the road is rough and tough." - ADP

29. "One of the benefits of knowledge is to straighten the path ahead of you." - ADP

30. "The best way to pass an exam is not to cram a subject, but it is to study and understand the subject." - ADP

31. "Some people will prefer something magical rather than something miraculous." - ADP

32. "Every miracle you will ever need is in God's voice." - ADP

33. "If you are a friend of God, it is easy for God to talk to you." - ADP

34. "Your life will always reflect what you know." - ADP

35. "The moment the spirit world sees the glow in you, that spirit world automatically takes you to the height you know." - ADP

36. "By a decision, Daniel decided to go up. He did not need an invitation." - ADP

37. "It is not enough to set your gaze on certain invitation or knowledge. You must make a decision and take action." - ADP

38. "There are times that people try to rise by their strength and

their skills, but there are those that when you look at their lives, you know that only God could have done this." - ADP

39. "God is in the business of changing the status of somebody." - ADP

40. "God takes no pleasure in your failure." - ADP

41. "God does almost nothing with your failure." - ADP

42. "Satan uses your failure to mock you and to mock God." - ADP

43. "When things do not happen the way God expects them to work, Satan laughs at you and God." - ADP

44. "God has the power to lift you!" - ADP

45. "If the force controlling your future, destiny, and glory appears to be stronger than your efforts, they are weaker than God's power." - ADP

46. "Supernatural lifting is when everything in the natural can do whatever it wants to do to keep you down, but it cannot hold you down." - ADP

47. "You have to be interested in it because God cannot help a man or woman who is not interested in his help." - ADP

48. "The source of a thing determines the status of a thing." - ADP

49. "Satan is not interested in you, but all he wants to do is to divide you with every single opportunity he has." - ADP

50. "Temptation is not a sin. Giving into temptation is what is sin." - ADP

51. "If you are not lifted, Satan uses your life as a bad example." - ADP

52. "Your father, God, wants to use your life as an advertisement

and an invitation to his other children that Satan is currently holding in captivity." - ADP

53. "Arise and shine! Whenever light comes, all of a sudden, people begin to rise!" - ADP

54. "God knows what to do with your life. It is your responsibility to cooperate with God." - ADP

55. "Satan likes to use your calamity as an advertisement and a tool for blackmail." - ADP

56. "God wants you to rise so that your rise will serve as a billboard and an invitation to tell his other children that the life is better out here." - ADP

57. "Everyone that sits with God has a place of honor." - ADP

58. "Do not come to God and then go to pigs." - ADP

59. "When you lack the right knowledge, you suffer terrible consequences." - ADP

60. "A person may never know the full expectation of God if they fail to align with that expectation." - ADP

61. "That individual will constantly suffer defeat." - ADP

62. "They are never able to turn their lives around due to that." - ADP

63. "No one ever comes out of a hole if they keep digging the hole." - ADP

64. "When it comes to changing your life and story, the lack of knowledge will keep a person stagnant." - ADP

65. "The battle begins when the devil realizes that you know that your captivity must end." - ADP

66. "Efforts will become futile and useless where vultures are

permitted to mess up your sacrifices." - ADP

67. "When Satan discovers that you are willing to become great the way God wants you to be, he begins to panic and looks for the very information needed to use against you." - ADP

68. "You must have the complete knowledge of the process of your life's journey." - ADP

69. "There are things that God will not tell you until you pass certain tests, but there are certain important details that God will not keep away from you." - ADP

70. "If you are going to excel and rise, you must transition beyond what you know to what God knows." - ADP

71. "Working with what you know is good and amazing, but knowing what God knows is incredible." - ADP

72. "That is where the worst warfare of your life begins." - ADP

73. "Money flows in the direction of a rise." – ADP

CHAPTER FOURTEEN

WINNING WITH GOD

*"Boldness, Obedience, and the
Power of Divine Revelation"*

Winning with God requires a unique blend of boldness, obedience, and divine revelation. God is calling you to be bold, not just in your actions but also in your faith. Boldness is stepping out of your comfort zone and trusting that God's strength empowers you to face any challenge. Joshua was commanded to be courageous as he led the Israelites into the Promised Land. Similarly, you are called to confront obstacles with faith and confidence, knowing God is by your side.

Obedience is equally vital in this journey; faithful obedience involves aligning your actions with God's will, even when it is complex or counterintuitive. When you follow God's commands, you position yourself to experience His blessings, so remember that partial obedience is not faithful obedience. Committing to walking in God's ways opens the door to His favor and guidance.

Wisdom Capsules

1. "Satan is the master orchestrator of destiny stagnation. He opens certain doors wide only to close them somewhere along

the line. People who do not follow the will and mind of God fall into traps of the enemy - and the enemy goes on rejoicing saying that even God cannot help them." - ADP

2. "In this life, it is impossible for there to ever be a problem or a challenge before the solution exists." - Exodus 15:24 TLB

3. "If only you will give God the chance to prove to you how loving, caring, powerful, and wise he is!" - ADP

4. "If only you will give him the chance to prove to you that his foolishness is wiser than your wisdom!" - ADP

5. "If only you will never allow your head to be wiser than God's heart for you." - ADP

6. "When you put your trust in humans who do not know God, they will hurt you, drop you, waste you, and mess you before you know it." - ADP

7. "When God is taking you on a journey, he is using Satan as a school for you - even when Satan thinks he is working against you." - ADP

8. "There are no risks of failure with God." - Psalm 62:2 TPT

9. "The only way you can win with God is to die before starting." - Esther 4:1610. "Any and everyone that learns how to win with God never loses to the devil and never goes down." - ADP

11. "Come to a place where Christianity is not a religion to you." - ADP

12. "A place where you understand that life is a real warfare." - ADP

13. "Like David, do not look for cheap victory. Look for lasting triumph - that the work of God in your life will outlive you." - ADP

14. "Understand that although the plan of Satan is real, the plan of God is more real, and the plan of God has a path. You cannot take your path and arrive at God's place! It is the path of God that brings you to the palace and the place God ordained for you." - ADP

15. "You will get there!" - ADP

16. "God has a plan, a path, and a place. The path of God will bring you to the palace." - ADP

17. "The plan of God requires the path of God. The path comes with a price. Those unwilling to find the path will always end up being defeated by the serpent, the adder, and the viper." - ADP

18. "Whatever your future holds can be seen in the past. You have a choice to choose if you want to win or lose." - ADP

19. "When you honor God, God takes care of the rest!" - ADP

20. "God's presence is our guarantee for safety, and it comes to those that honor him. It is a price that you pay." - Psalm 23:4 TLB

21. "You have a choice in this journey whether to be lifted or to be dropped and stagnant." - ADP

22. "If things are not going right, you can reverse it - regardless of the mistake." - ADP

23. "Taking away the cobwebs without killing the spider makes you a fool - but killing the spider comes with a price." - ADP

24. "Why should you die with your enemy? Why should you die the death of your adversary?" - ADP

25. "Prove to the devil that God is your father!" - Psalm 3:2 TPT

26. "Do not give the enemy room to blaspheme or laugh at God." - ADP

27. "Let your life glorify God to the last beat of your heart. Jesus

has to be glorified." - ADP

28. "No matter how ugly things look, ashes become beauty when God takes over!" - 2 Samuel 24:24-25 TLB

29. "Satan will make you do everything else other than what God wants you to do." - ADP

30. "There is no plague or defeat in your life that cannot be stopped - but the choice is yours!" - ADP

31. "Doing the will of God is one of the most challenging things, but the moment you do it successfully, you incapacitate and defeat the devil." - ADP

32. "God is a God of process! People are windows!" - Isaiah 8:19 KJV

33. "The devil defeats you by attacking the part of you that is eager to obey God by using the other part of you that is lazy." - Matthew 26:40-41 TPT/MSG

34. "What you say is what matters. If you fail to say more than the enemies are saying, you will never become more than the enemies are saying. You must say more than the enemies say because words are the major forces in deciding things in the spirit world. Your words will create your world!" - ADP

35. "Supplication is prayer. Supplication is the submission of your application for a change of status." - Psalm 3:3-4 TPT

36. "Anything that keeps you away from Mount Zion will keep you away from the presence of God. There is something that unlocks the presence of God when you come to his holy presence." - ADP

37. "Heights that happen by miracles can only be sustained by intelligence." - ADP

38. "Where there are no miracles, intelligence well applied can

take you to heights that miracles cannot take you to." - ADP

39. "The moment you can gather the condition, and you begin to work on yourself to meet the condition, you become the solution." - Acts 16:25-28 TPT

40. "It is always better to ask God about the condition required for the position you are applying for." - ADP

41. "You know you are on track with God by the constancy of instructions." - ADP

42. "The evidence of your experience is in your ability to stick to the flight instructions." - ADP

43. "Ask God for instruction - 'What are the instructions for my life?'" - ADP

44. "It does not matter how desperate you are for a change of status, if God answers your prayers for height without giving you instruction, you will fall." - Psalm 32:8 AMP

45. "You know God is instructing you when you begin to notice irritation at the instruction received. Suppose Satan successfully gives you an irritation towards the instructions God gives to you. In that case, he will successfully give you an imitation of your destiny and the purpose of God for you. Satan likes it when you are always confused about the will of God." - ADP

46. "Pursuing destiny is demanding, challenging, and naturally difficult. No instruction of God does not come with high demands - you successfully meet the demands by receiving multiplied grace." - Philippians 2:12; Luke 19:22 TPT; 2 Corinthians 12:9 TPT

47. "Grace is that spiritual grease that makes the journey to the top easier - it makes difficult things look easy - it enables you to do difficult things easily." - ADP

48. "When you are weak, the grace of God makes you powerful

so that you are never out of the ability to obey God. Every great destiny rides on the wings of obedience." - Isaiah 1:19 TLB

49. "Real destiny requires a high price, and you pay the high price by receiving grace from God. Loving God will make you come to him and ask him for grace to do what he has asked you to do." - ADP

50. "Apply for the Father's help to represent the Father and fulfill his will on earth boldly. Submit your application for a change of status, height, situation, condition, and position." - ADP

51. "Where there is no boldness, there will be no rise. Even if you rise by a miracle, there are things at the top that desire to eat you up - you need to be bold." - ADP

52. "Satan loves a man or woman that is cold. He fears a man/woman that is bold." - ADP

53. "Boldness is the combination of four factors: relationship with God, the covenant factor, the revelation of who God is to you, spirit empowerment, and covenant practices." - ADP

54. "Anything that wants to destroy you will block your heart from a heart to pray." - ADP

55. "Do not go with your excitement, go with divine revelation." - ADP

CHAPTER FIFTEEN

STAND OUT TO SHINE FORTH

*"From Potential To Power And
Unleashing Your Unique Calling
And Building A Legacy"*

Y ou were created for a purpose and a unique destiny that reflects the glory of God. Each of us has a specific role in His grand design, and understanding that place is essential to realizing our potential. The beauty of your destiny lies in the gifts and talents God has bestowed upon you, waiting to be unveiled in the world. To shine means to illuminate the darkness around you, and your destined place is where that light can radiate most effectively. Think of a lighthouse; it serves no purpose on dry land and must be positioned on the coast to guide ships to shore safely. Likewise, you must be spiritually, emotionally, and physically in the right place to fulfill your calling to shine forth. Remember that challenges may arise in your pursuit of destiny, but these are often stepping stones rather than obstacles.

Wisdom Capsules

1. "Most people are the witches and wizards sabotaging their

destiny. Understand that the uniqueness of your life and destiny requires your respect." - ADP

2. "If a flawed man allows God to work on him, God will display him on the floor. God will not work you despite you. He will work with you because of you. He will never showcase a flawed stone." - ADP

3. "The teachings of God can chisel and cleanse your life if you allow God." - John 15:3 KJV - ADP

4. "What makes a believer a murderer is when they begin to hate the truth. Truth cleanses a person. When the word comes, it is meant to cleanse you, but if your heart's not open to the word, it will irritate you." - John 8:44 tlb; John 15:3 KJV - ADP

5. "A liar is not someone who just did not tell the truth. A liar loves anything that does not place a demand on them, especially in their pursuit of the destiny God has for them." - ADP

6. "There is nothing God wants to do in your life that will not place a demand on you. No one responds to the demands of God and does not become a highly placed person on earth. Make up your mind to walk with God!" - ADP

7. "You will always need God's intervention. There is something God wants to do with your life. Recognize that! Do not allow the devil to infect your mind." - ADP

8. "You must be intentional about purpose. Be intentional when it comes to living. Do not live like a loser. Live your life like a miracle going somewhere to happen - like a champion." - ADP

9. "Live with the consciousness of purpose. Declare, 'I am a carrier of destiny, so my purpose is to reveal the magnanimity of God's kindness to humanity.'" - ADP

10. "Live with passion. When passion is taken out of purpose, purpose becomes a burden that will eventually become a

liability. Ensure that you are not mediocre. Be passionate about your calling. Study to show yourself approved of God." - Colossians 3:23-24 - ADP

11. "Understand that the world is dark. That is why you are here to be God's light. You will never stand out if you think as everyone thinks. You cannot change the world you are called to be like. You are called to be light - do not admire darkness." - John 1:5 amp - ADP

12. "No matter the situation, live with the consciousness that you are the solution, not the problem - the miracle, not the obstacle of bad news - the answer, not the question." - ADP

13. "When God begins to work on you, you must understand that you are the light, and you must never give darkness the chance to absorb you." - ADP

14. "When giving to God, you cannot give him a bowl. You have to give him the whole." - ADP

15. "The secret of the power of my altar is that I do not hold back anything for God. God uses me as a distribution center." - ADP

16. "I keep working to raise people." - ADP

17. "When you see a man who has humbled lions, do not try to cross his path." - ADP

18. "Only fools doubt proofs. If you follow God's instruction through me, your life can never be insignificant. The evidence will be surely seen." - ADP

19. "The secret of my power is my altar. What is powering my life cannot be contaminated." - ADP

20. "You cannot use passivity to correct negativity." - ADP

21. "There is a level of spiritual aggression, passion, and consistency that is required to correct negativity." - ADP

22. "I cannot be canceled. I know God!" - ADP

23. "Your future is in the scripture. If you can find it in the scripture, you can feature your future." - ADP

24. "I am anointed but instructed." - ADP

25. "If a plane is taking off and the engine is messed up, that is a dangerous flight." - ADP

26. "Carelessness will kill you faster than 300 demons." - ADP

27. "Things unseen leave the mind un-shattered. Chase and see what will take you up." - ADP

28. "Strong men are not built or strengthened off of smooth roads." - ADP

29. "Give your children things they gravitate towards - things that will improve them. Your children will learn from one example more than a thousand explanations." - ADP

30. "Great people are self-starters. They need little or no encouragement, and they go for what they want." - ADP

31. "Learners are earners." - ADP

32. "Do not be a stranger in the field of greatness. Humble yourself and be a learner. Learners are earners." - ADP

33. "Have mercy on your brain and do not feed your brain with social media shorts and reels. Your brain is shaped by whatever you constantly feed yourself with, and in return, it shapes your life." - ADP

34. "I am not crazy about money because I have exchanged money for power. I know that power will bring money." - ADP

35. "We all have grace, but I work hard. I do not give credit to my work, but I give credit to grace. My grace makes sense because I work." - ADP

36. "Humility is not in the bling. It is in your content." - ADP

37. "Never electrocute what you are meant to electrify. Your relationship will be boring if there is no electricity in it." - ADP

38. "Trying to be right is not my motive. All of my attempts are to ensure your enemies do not laugh at you because they are waiting to laugh at you." - ADP

39. "People make excuses because nothing is burning inside." - ADP

40. "I may be a wind that likes to blow nice breeze, but I am like a thunder. I like to roar." - ADP

41. "Everything you do, you are building part of history. When history is told, what side of it will you be on?" - ADP

42. "An abused mind will always end up in poverty and penury." - ADP

43. "Your dominion is too dangerous!" - ADP

44. "Reaction against mediocrity is what empowers you for excellence." - ADP

45. "Reaction against the present is a major key to creating a desired future." - ADP

46. "People will treat you with ignominy until you give them the reason to treat you with dignity." - ADP

47. "The reason is because you have not shown them the greatness within you. People will invest in a potential event. When people see that you are a potential warning to happen, the tendency of investing in you is high, but if you allow yourself to be one of those laggers, the Amalekites will erase and erode you." - ADP

48. "When you connect to where you are from, what is in your

source begins to flow in your life." - ADP

49. "If you do not cultivate your atmosphere, people will contaminate your atmosphere." - ADP

50. "When you see beauty growing, water it." - ADP

51. "I would rather be down than be helped by the wrong person." - ADP

52. "When you do not see my face, check who is watching your back." - ADP

53. "Do your best. Keep God first!" - ADP

54. "Every time you invest time with God, God will give time in return." - ADP

55. "You must never speak based on your bank account. You must speak based on your word account." - ADP

56. "If a small boy with a big God is leading you, you better make yourself a small child." - ADP

57. "I would rather honor and obey God, not knowing the outcome, than ignore God and become the victim. When I make a God move, I must watch out for the vultures and protect my sacrifice, effort, and commitment to God from the vultures." - ADP

58. "The more of God you reveal, the more like God you become. The more of God you give, the more of God you get. The more of God you get, the more of God you become." - ADP

59. "People ask me, 'Apostle, what are you using?' I say, 'I am using craziness.' I am wildly crazy. None of my mates can catch me." - ADP

60. "Never get tired of doing what is required to take you higher." - ADP

61. "Every human being is a leper and every leper needs a helper." - Luke 7:38-39 tpt - ADP

62. "I can take your time but I will give you your life." - ADP

63. "You are good for the throne. Why settle for the trash?" - ADP

CHAPTER SIXTEEN

THE COMMANDED BLESSING

*Unlocking divine favor and
sustained success*

God's commanded blessing in your life is a powerful affirmation of His love and purpose for you. He has already established blessings that are meant to overtake you, bringing divine favor and sustained success. Deuteronomy 28:2 teaches that these blessings come when you listen to and obey God's voice. This obedience opens the door to a life filled with His favor, where His plans for you unfold. You might sometimes feel weak or helpless, especially when faced with challenges or setbacks. However, it is vital to remember that God does not define you by your circumstances; He defines you by His promises. You are not powerless. You are a child of the Most High God, and His strength empowers you. Philippians 4:13 reminds you, "I can do all things through Christ which strengtheneth me."

Wisdom Capsules

1. "The blessing is not material. The blessing has the power to sustain your life and secure your future." - ADP

2. "When steps are miscalculated and blessings are invoked or involved, the miscalculated steps become calculated steps." - ADP

3. "Whatever you do, do not despise the blessing. It is costly to pay for a missed blessing." - ADP

4. "The blessing of God is the maker of men. The blessing of God is the force that rearranges a man's life." - ADP

5. "Do not give in to Esau. Keep on fighting for the blessing. Esau despise spiritual things." - ADP

6. "His quest and craving for spiritual things turned him into a temporal object of mockery. When you are an object of mockery, wait until your story is over. Life is in phases; every phase will end to open a new phase for you." - ADP

7. "Nothing excites God like a spiritually excited person." - ADP

8. "You cannot be a weakling and expect to make sense of your life. It takes a lion heart to have a lion share." - Joshua 1:6 - ADP

9. "Do not try to be courageous if you are not strong. Greatness is not for the weak." - Joshua 1:6 - ADP

10. "Power with God is the blessing of God." - ADP

11. "Be desperate for the blessing. It is the key to proliferation and sustenance." - ADP

12. "There are some people that are so blessed because their primary assignment is to ensure that those who are supposed to perish do not perish." - ADP

13. "The broken most times become masters at mending." - ADP

14. "The reason we have the poor amongst us is for the wise to rise." - ADP

15. "The first evidence of a spiritual blessing is a spiritual

covering." - ADP

16. "Curses empower a person to fail." - ADP

17. "Understand that God has a reason for training you the way He trains you." - ADP

18. "The blessing is more than material things. Blessing is different from making. Blessing involves a process of giving. Making involves a process of melting, bending, and breaking you to train and make you into who you need to be." - ADP

19. "God is making you the shortcut to people's greatness." - ADP

20. "God will put you in a place where some things you are not expecting will come your way. The blessing forces everywhere to be a bank." - ADP

21. "No matter what it costs you, labor to generate the anointing. This is the blessing of God that ensures that wherever you show up, miracles will begin to happen." - ADP

22. "Satan will never offer you what was not yours in the first place. That which God gave to man was what Satan offered to the Son of Man." - ADP

23. "When it comes to your blessing, cast Satan out. Do not negotiate with him or listen to him. He comes to steal. God is saying to you that you are almost there. Pass the test!" - ADP

24. "A convenient obedience is not obedience. Every demand from God will put you in a place where your heart will shake." - ADP

25. "If Satan makes you rich, you and your generation will never be able to pay the price." - ADP

26. "When a blessing rests upon you, it releases strength and favor to the entire city." - Proverbs 11:10 TPT - ADP

27. "Many have received blessings that did not rest. As a result, they have not found rest." - ADP

28. "When the blessing rests upon a man, it releases strength and favor." - Proverbs 11:10 TPT - ADP

29. "The blessing ensures that your end is beautiful. Fight to get the blessing!" - ADP

30. "Anything you use God's strength to fight for the blessing, you may end up getting it, but you will limp at the end." - ADP

31. "The blessed one who is releasing strength and makes others stronger." - ADP

32. "Use the strength God gives you to distribute the blessing! That you feel strength does not mean you should go and fight. Strength means to settle and strategize. The blessing releases strength." - ADP

33. "With the carrier of the blessing comes an atmosphere. The atmosphere releases strength." - ADP

34. "When you have a rested blessing on you and meet another person with a rested blessing, your baby will leap for joy!" - ADP

35. "When you become weary, you start fighting the people God ordained to help you. It is a sign of foolishness. Using the strength obtained from the blessing to fight the bless-er." - ADP

36. "When you embrace the one releasing strength, favor is released. Winning without fighting!" - ADP

37. "Favor will make the custodian of the materials look at you with high value, appreciation, the needed compassion, and excitement. They know that you carry something." - ADP

38. "What you cannot get fighting, favor gives it with ease." - ADP

39. "God wants to demonstrate His greatness, but He also wants to demonstrate His love and kindness." - ADP

40. "Spiritual things are powerful, and if you are not intentional, you will become a victim of spiritual things. When you are intentional, you will find yourself soaring." - ADP

41. "The commanded blessing = when an authorized person who has the right to a blessing gives you the password to access their treasures." - Isaiah 45:3 TLB - ADP

42. "Because of the commanded blessing, when people see you winning, they do not know that you have been given teeth. What stops them feeds you. What scares them is what you chew!" - ADP

43. "Wisdom enables you to navigate through life with fewer struggles or complications - avoiding useless battles." - ADP

44. "Wisdom gives you access to spiritual things and gives you access to the spirit world of other people." - ADP

45. "The commanded blessing brings wisdom to the blessed." - ADP

46. "If you have no idea, your greatness will always be locked up somewhere." - ADP

47. "God dislikes it when you do not give Him glory or attach importance to what He is doing. If you take that which God is doing for granted, you will pay for it." - Malachi 2:2-3 - ADP

48. "When the commanded blessing is upon you, you do not have to be afraid of what God has given to you. It removes competition from your life. God will always give you an edge and put you ahead." - ADP

49. "Never think that things you trivialize cannot ruin your life." - ADP

50. "The reason you are a child of God is to be a shining light to your world." - ADP

51. "When the commanded blessing comes upon a person, it corrects many things. It is like a dew that comes upon wet dry grass and makes it grow, even if there is no rain." - ADP

52. "True rest = serving God with your life and strength. When you give God your strength, He will mesmerize you." - ADP

53. "The commanded blessing is the blessing that receives direction from God and knows how to work the earth - establishing things in such a way that things will come to you and take care of you even if you do not work." - ADP

54. "One of the keys to the commanded blessing is obedience." - ADP

55. "Foolishness makes you a victim of bewitchment. Bewitchment brings you to a place of foolishness." - ADP

56. "Vashti was more beautiful than Esther, but Esther was more powerful than Vashti. It is not the beautiful one that wins but the powerful one!" - ADP

57. "When it comes to the prophetic, if all you know is to prophesy, you are a weak prophet. You have to know spiritual technicalities." - ADP

58. "Esther had an altar of prayer, fasting, and sacrifice continually, and Mordecai was her teacher." - ADP

59. "When pressure comes, the real you comes out." - ADP

60. "Wherever there is an altar, there are representatives." - ADP

61. "When the blessings of God are at work in a man's life, the blessings make his children influential." - ADP

62. "Do not joke with people that respect altars. Whether they

are good or bad altars." - ADP

63. "Do not allow your altar to be weak that it loses its ability to influence your cloud or atmosphere." - ADP

64. "There are powers that want to undermine God, so God wants to brag with people like you and me." - ADP

65. "Your highest wisdom is to let God be the God of your life and to follow God all the days of your life." - ADP

66. "Wrong prophecies can be corrected when destiny altars are repaired and the destiny is commanded." - ADP

67. "Until you leave this earth, you must service the altar and keep it alive. The laws of the altar demands that the altar must never go out." - ADP

68. "When your life begins to respond to the power and fragrance of your altar, your battles look/seem small or non-existent." - ADP

69. "The commanded blessing corrects a person's atmosphere. It is like dew upon Mount Hermon." - ADP

70. "When the blessing of God is developing a person's life and the person ignores the spiritual exercises and practices needed, they will find that the blessing given loses strength." - ADP

71. "The good thing God gives to you can lose its strength if not handled well." - ADP

72. "You cannot be a game player with God and expect to win the game. The smartest thing to do is never to play games with God." - ADP

73. "When God tells you 'I am lifting you,' you tell God 'I am holding on to you.'" - ADP

74. "God's people are supposed to be marked by God. We are not

supposed to be victims of what others are victims of." - ADP

75. "You never go down following God. It may cost you more, but it is worth it." - ADP

76. "God says, 'I have given you rest.' So do not panic." - ADP

77. "The days we live in are susceptible days." - ADP

78. "God is raising a generation of men and women that will be lovers and worshippers of God in spirit and truth!" - ADP

79. "Come to a place where you are truly humble so that you can open up to God and allow God to make you who He wants you to be." - ADP

80. "Do not go through God's drive-through car wash service. You may pay less both in cash and kind, but when you go through His detailed service and pay with your time and in cash, what comes back to you is value and excellence." - ADP

CHAPTER SEVENTEEN

THE POWER OF
THE BLESSING

*Rising Above Challenges
with God's Favor*

God's blessings are designed to change your life for good, and that's why the Bible says in Ephesians 1:3 that we are already blessed with all spiritual blessings in Christ. This is not just a promise for the future; it is a present reality that should impact your daily life. When you truly grasp the magnitude of these blessings, you will begin to see their potential to reshape your life and circumstances.

God's blessings are multifaceted; they can come in joy, peace, health, provision, relationships, and opportunities. Each blessing serves as a reminder of His love and faithfulness.

Wisdom Capsules

1. "Depression is an indication of distance from God. One of the evidences of closeness to God is joy unspeakable - full of glory." - James 1:2 KJV - ADP

2. "Everything about your life has entered into a new season. Your life will experience divine refreshing." - ADP

3. "To be blessed = to be empowered to succeed against all odds, adversities, adversities, and traps. It is the eliminator of sorrow." - ADP

4. "The blessing is direct access to the protection and preservation of God." - 2 Samuel 15:31 KJV - ADP

5. "The blessing is magnetic. It is meant to make things beautiful." - ADP

6. "Satan likes beautiful things not because he likes beautiful things but because he is a destroyer of beautiful things. So when you are being blessed, ensure that your blessing is protected from sorrow." - ADP

7. "Ask God for manifested blessing. He said that from this day, He will bless you." - Haggai 2:17-19 TLB - ADP

8. "When you are blessed, life cannot enslave you. No one can tell you that you are cursed. Instead, you will have slaves." - ADP

9. "In life, weak people are kings and queens of blackmail. If you trust the wrong person, they will use what they know against you. Sometimes, it causes sorrow." - Proverbs 10:18 TPT - ADP

10. "There are times when your life is easier and better when you can identify an enemy and know who you cannot trust." - ADP

11. "If you are determined to rise by the blessing, you must eliminate every sorrow. Sorrow comes when foes pretend to be friends." - ADP

12. "Sorrow comes like a friend. People who are sponsors of sorrow or have evil plots succeed because you give it room." - ADP

13. "The measure with which you measure for others is the same way others will use to measure for you." - ADP

14. "When humans decide to become the source of your sorrow,

if you are blessed, that sorrow will be eradicated." - ADP

15. "Develop yourself to the new you that God is raising. Build yourself, grow, and become who God is making you. Leave your signature, not your stench. Become that vanilla flower, not a skunk." - ADP

16. "God authorizes you to take what He has for you." - ADP

17. "If you are empty-hearted, you will be absent-minded. Absent-minded people are those who talk before they leap." - Proverbs 10:19 - ADP

18. "Sorrow rides on the wings of useless talks, so if you do not have what to say, say nothing." - Proverbs 10:19 - ADP

19. "Talkative are harvesters of sorrow." - Proverbs 17:28 NLT - ADP

20. "Build yourself. Be a man/woman of substance." - ADP

21. "Keep your heart pure. Make up your mind to be hungry for pure truth. Be excited about the fact that knowing the truth will always make you free." - ADP

22. "Error is the chief sponsor of sorrow. Mistakes are moves that are wrongly taken, but if mistakes are not addressed, they bring about error. Error brings slavery." - ADP

23. "When God wants to punish a person, He keeps the person in the dark." - ADP

24. "Prophets are agents of intervention called by God to bring profit into your life and to make your life profitable. They are carriers of profit. When they show up in your life, sorrows are eliminated." - ADP

25. "You must learn to challenge God's blessing in your life and for your life, else you will never maximize the blessings of God." - ADP

26. "It is possible to have the best life if only you master the art of referring your life's challenges to the blessings of God upon your life or your lineage." - ADP

27. "Blessings are spiritual specialists that release the power, aroma, and fortune needed to give you the life you desire or the life God has promised you." - ADP

28. "When you master certain spiritual things, you will begin to rule." - ADP

29. "If you do not show excitement over your redemption, it is withdrawn from you. Excitement validates the license of believers." - ADP

30. "When your greatest pride is in the life you used to have or in the blessing you used to have, that is the spirit of the tail." - ADP

31. "Every month ought to be a harvest season." - ADP

32. "When you find that the spirit of the tail is attacking you, you refer the spirit of the tail to the blessing of the head." - ADP

33. "When you refer your battles to the right specialist - and you know the right things to do and you take a position - over some time, your life will begin to work again." - ADP

34. "What Satan hates the most is for you to catch the secret and unction to being anointed. You must fight for the blessing. You must decide to be blessed and make sense of your life." - ADP

35. "When God says 'I will bless you and make your name great and you will be a blessing,' He means He is establishing something within you that will continually flow so that others can take from it." - ADP

36. "When God places a blessing on you, good things grow." - ADP

37. "When God sends the showers, He will cause your crops to

grow." - ADP

38. "Personalize this. Declare: 'The blessings on my life will cause good things to grow wherever I go.'" - ADP

39. "Do not be afraid. Make that next move!" - ADP

40. "Whatever you and I will ever need is available." - ADP

41. "When they show their foolishness, answer with wisdom." - ADP

42. "When they show their stupidity, answer with dignity." - ADP

43. "Part of the benefit of choosing the blessing is that the blessing comes with a pact - a peace pact. This peace travels with you all your life. It is a double-edged sword." - ADP

44. "When you ignore simple things or do not know how to navigate through simple things, you find your life complicated. Follow the simple instructions - the simple things - so that God can handle that which is complex." - ADP

45. "There is an aspect of your story that people do not know. That is the God factor! It's a God story." - Romans 4:1-3 MSG - ADP

46. "The prophetic is the shortest cut to the fastest answers you desire. It is foolishness to be philosophical when you are depending on the prophetic." - ADP

47. "God is about to make you an extraordinary achiever." - ADP

48. "The new season of your life is a season of budding, blossoming, and ripe fruits. No more sour fruits. You now have access to ripe fruits." - ADP

CHAPTER EIGHTEEN

Destiny And Divine Instruction

U nlocking the Power of Obedience
Understanding your destiny is crucial, but your ability to heed divine instruction is even more critical. You must have realized that God's guidance is the roadmap to fulfilling His purpose for your life. Proverbs 4:7 is one scripture that emphasizes the importance of wisdom and understanding, reminding us that acquiring these qualities is foundational for success. When you ignore God's instructions, you will go off course, ultimately hindering your journey toward destiny.

Disregarding divine guidance always leads to detrimental consequences. Think about the Israelites. They wandered in the wilderness for forty years because they refused God's instructions. Their disobedience delayed their entry into the Promised Land and caused them to miss out on the abundant life God had prepared for them.

Wisdom Capsules

1. "If you know the instructions of God but miss the timings, you will miss it all." - ADP

2. "Individuals who learn to align with divine instruction end up creating their destinies." - ADP

3. "There is always a simple solution to complex situations. Only the ridiculous can access the miraculous." - ADP

4. "Most people miss God and His benefits because sometimes He gives them instructions that do not make sense. If it doesn't make sense but it makes good, watch out for the sense in it." - ADP

5. "God will always tell you to do things contrary to your human strength." - ADP

6. "Everything that functions on Earth responds to sound. Certain things will never become yours until you respond to a sound." - ADP

7. "Since the fall of man, sounds that echo into man's destiny has been the sound of sorrow, so man had to struggle to get things done." - ADP

8. "Sound creates energy or sucks out energy." - ADP

9. "Your new phase is depending and waiting for your sound. Your real sound is not the sound you make when the trumpet sounds... It is the one you generate in your time of quiet walk because the quiet walk is the weary one." - ADP

10. "There are people who are children of God but do not have an understanding of times and seasons." - ADP

11. "You must come to a place where you are sensitive to seasons of your life." - ADP

12. "When God calls you to do great things, resolve in your heart to serve God His way and be determined to not give in to the voices of those whose dedication is not contagious." - ADP

13. "When God calls you to do great things, you must have strength and the ability to sustain." - ADP

14. "People have a revelation of what God said, but they never become what God said they will be because they are insensitive to the requirements and actions required to enter into their new place!" - ADP

15. "Look out of those of us who are stupid enough to respect the rules of the spirit world, and you will find that we are the strongest who keep going when everyone else is weary." - ADP

16. "To carry the Ark of God, you must bear the burden/pain of walking in the anointing and the price of serving God." - ADP

17. "Sound affects the mind. When a man's mind is affected by divine sound, creativity comes alive." - ADP

18. "Do not try to divide the waters if you have not carried the Ark on your shoulders. If you cannot carry the Ark, follow those who carry it." - ADP

19. "God likes to show off. He is the master of bad things. Evil things cannot intimidate Him!" - ADP

20. "A wise person will see the fact that God is giving a ridiculous instruction at a ridiculous season for the miraculous to manifest." - ADP

21. "If someone has not decided what they want in life, let them be. You are not God!" - ADP

22. "God does not make investments where there is instability. An unstable mind is an unworthy investment." - ADP

23. "Declare 'I'm set.'" - ADP

24. "That is the mentality needed for the prosperity promised. This mentality releases creativity and ideas." - ADP

25. "Projectional reasoning is the engaging of your mind to engage a future by planning." - ADP

26. "A motivational mind is a mind sensitized into positive motion by positive information." - ADP

27. "Life only keeps you at your level." - ADP

28. "What have you done to personalize your prophecy?" - ADP

29. "The moment your mind receives new information, your soul gets excited and strength comes to you." - ADP

30. "When you are wise, you can pull down any resistance." - ADP

31. "When you are set, this mentality is transformational. It can change your perception of life so that you can get the right results at once." - ADP

32. "When the blessing of God is upon your mind, He gives you a mindset of creativity for prosperity." - ADP

33. "When you are set, this mentality is transformational. It gives you the ability to vision. Everything you create in your mind begins to manifest." - ADP

34. "As the carrier of the Ark, when you carry God's presence, you dominate nations." - ADP

35. "Ark on your shoulder = presence of your feet." - ADP

36. "You must decide to cross over to the other side. The voice of your choice should choke the voice of what comes to you by default." - ADP

37. "Choose life. Choose to win. Be determined to win. Choose to be strong. Choose to be better. Choose to cross over to the other

side." - ADP

38. "Generate so much unction that crossing-over, which seems intimidating, bows to your feet." - ADP

39. "The more you stay in God's presence, the more power you generate and the less effort you have to put into life's battle to win big." - ADP

40. "Your outcome is a product of your personal choice." - ADP

41. "You must decide to act when God is speaking. Do not wait." - ADP

42. "When people do not understand your move, make moves. Decide in your heart that you will be either the envy of your friend or the most respected of your friends." - ADP

43. "You have been waiting for God, but God says you have been carrying Me all these years. Deep your feet into that which you desire!" - ADP

44. "Talk to God. Listen to God. Prepare yourself for success. Agree with someone who wants to see you succeed." - ADP

45. "The priest cannot carry the power and presence if they do not want to carry the Ark on their shoulder." - ADP

46. "Your value and respect for the bearers of God's Ark will determine the benefit that comes to you when you cross to the other side." - ADP

47. "I am crossing over into the promised good land. I am going beyond the resistance and the intimidation of the Jordan River. I am going to the place of progress. I will see the result of all the greatness and power you have been showing us." - ADP

48. "The help that comes from the sanctuary responds to the sacrifice you have made in the sanctuary." - ADP

49. "It is so simple to be blessed by God, yet some people complicate their lives." - ADP

50. "Irresponsible Christianity is the reason for the decadence you see in the church today." - ADP

51. "Do not cross Jordan when everything is calm. The key is simple obedience." - ADP

52. "In the eyes of God, partial obedience is equal to disobedience." - ADP

53. "You miss out on the best God has for you when you try to worship your needs." - ADP

54. "When you win, Satan can only defeat you by creating a gap. The moment to start advancing, Satan starts bringing the things you choose." - ADP

55. "The moment you know you are advancing, do not make space. Make the needed sacrifice to fill any gap." - ADP

56. "There ought to be a level of relationship with God where your altar is so alive that it begins to answer questions you do not understand - answers that go into your future to tackle complications. Ensuring your life enjoys the favor of God." - ADP

57. "No matter how positive a prophecy is, if you do not take care of tragedy, the force that pulls people down always seems stronger than the force that pulls people up." - ADP

58. "Some people are miserable today because they are wasters of divine investment. It is difficult for God to get them to act honorably in advancing His kingdom despite all the years of investment." - ADP

59. "Why should God set you up to do destiny when you know the level of His investments in you?" - ADP

60. "There are instructions and guidelines to everyone's destiny.

Satan loves it when you constantly violate the guidelines to your destiny." - ADP

61. "There are many people today that God cannot talk to because His voice often doesn't make sense. So God will have to set them up." - ADP

62. "Why should God set you up to have you do His will?" - ADP

63. "How much pain, sorrow, and tragedy do you need to align with God's purpose? What is your calling and your purpose?" - ADP

64. "Your relationship with God determines the strength of your altar." - ADP

65. "If your hair grows, use the best hair product. That is called satisfying your altar. Ensure you do everything not to allow contradictory patterns." - ADP

66. "No matter how smart and strong you are as a king, if you do not have the backing of a spiritual priest, no matter how much you win, you will end up in disaster." - ADP

67. "To be well trained is to be taught how to serve God His way, not your way - to know what is required of you" - ADP

CHAPTER NINETEEN

THE POWER OF DIVINE INSTRUCTIONS

Unlocking Shortcuts to Miracles

Divine instructions act as shortcuts and paths leading to accelerated success, healing, and even provision when needed. When you listen and obey, you open the door to miracles you may have thought impossible. God's instructions often come in unexpected ways, through His Word, the counsel of others, or even through the still, small voice of the Holy Spirit. Your responsibility is to remain sensitive to His leading!

1. "If you are not protected, you are zero regardless of who you are or what you have." - ADP

2. "There is a place that you stand in with God where what destroys others cannot destroy you." - ADP

3. "You must learn to know with whom and where you are connected with/to. Never go down like a chicken." - ADP

4. "If you do not understand your authority and connection, you will become a victim." - ADP

5. "Do not take the time you are supposed to spend honoring God and give it to something else. Have a change of mind." - ADP

6. "Seek the way to serve God in an honorable way. There is no time invested in God's presence that is a waste." - ADP

7. "You will never see the great power of God until you start honoring God with and in the little things." - ADP

8. "You will be shocked what God will do through you if you give Him the chance to do it." - ADP

9. "Whenever you are faced with anyone's problems, remember that you are the solution." - ADP

10. "God is not calling you to be so powerful with yourself alone - just connect with God." - ADP

11. "The outcome of God's blessing is the refusal to leave you where your blessing met you." - ADP

12. "You know you are blessed when you have received a word over your life that says, 'Your life will not be the same.'" - ADP

13. "You know the blessing is working when you no longer live where you have been in life." - ADP

14. "The blessing of God forbids decrease, but in case there is a need to reshuffle your life, God will take you through a route that looks like decrease but is not decrease." - ADP

15. "Sometimes when God is re-routing your life, and it looks as if He is reducing you, He is not reducing you; He is re-routing you and getting ready to multiply you." - ADP

16. "Be expectant because God said your latter end will greatly increase. God is saying this is the lowest you will ever be!" - ADP

17. "The gift of a pure heart comes from God." - ADP

18. "It is never God's will for you to be insignificant. It is an abuse

of grace and blessing for the best to end up as an insignificant person." - ADP

19. "God wants you to be blessed now and forever." - ADP

20. "Going through all you are going through is a sign of being chosen by God." - ADP

21. "If you do not master the art of navigation, everything you go through will end up as a waste." - ADP

22. "If you cannot apply your life experiences to the reason God gave you life, it is useless." - ADP

23. "But if you master how to navigate correctly, you will soon realize that your going-through is working together for your good." - ADP

24. "Your going-through (your experiences) works for you if you learn how to connect with God's purpose." - ADP

25. "Trust is earned. Joseph vetted his brothers before he revealed himself to them." - ADP

26. "When God allows you to go through anything, eventually He wants that your experience is converted into tools in His hands so that you can affect the lives of people with the work of God in your hands." - ADP

27. "The real blessing that lasts is the blessing that is spread abroad." - ADP

28. "When God decides to bless a family, He picks an individual." - ADP

29. "If you respect your local level, you will soon become a global force." - ADP

30. "When your name becomes a force to be reckoned with, people will bless themselves in your name." - ADP

31. "Great people talk about great ideas and opportunities. Small people talk about other people and their failures." - ADP

32. "You are not the failure police." - ADP

33. "You may think you are strong, but little do you know that it is God that has been and still is covering your shame." - ADP

34. "If God removes His protection from you, you will see how foolish you are." - ADP

35. "You are destined to be a generational blessing, not a curse. Your life is meant to help people get better." - ADP

36. "Pride will make a person waste the blessings of God." - ADP

37. "The strength we have is God's grace and mercy." - ADP

38. "There is no strong man; there are only helped men." - ADP

39. "The purpose of the blessing is for you to have influence, power, and success that people will bless themselves in your name." - ADP

40. "Water refreshes. Honey satisfies. Prophetic declarations accelerate destiny." - ADP

41. "Most delays lead to satanic alternatives, making the very best of the best fall into satanic traps." - ADP

42. "You must be ready for the increase God is bringing. It is happening all at once." - ADP

43. "You must realize that Satan has been robbing you for a long time." - ADP

44. "There is no shortcut in life until you find the right shortcut. Everything requires a process." - ADP

45. "Every time you follow due process, you end up with the right product." - ADP

46. "Due process takes time to mature and connect for it to manifest." - ADP

47. "Strength does not come by accident. It comes by practice." - ADP

48. "Make sense while you have time. No matter how short the time is, make sense of your life." - ADP

49. "There is a level of strength required for you to fulfill destiny." - ADP

50. "Why do you need the shortcut?" - ADP

51. "Why do you need the prophetic?" - ADP

52. "The prophetic gives you access to the shortcuts for legal use." - ADP

53. "Every human on Earth is governed by certain laws that rule the universe." - ADP

54. "Every time you seek to understand God before you obey God, you will miss many things." - ADP

55. "Never allow your plans to supersede the plans of God or your spiritual authority." - ADP

56. "For you to successfully master spiritual things, you must have been consistent for at least twenty years or so - then explosion with stability happens." - ADP

57. "Otherwise, you have to take the prophetic route - the shortcut." - ADP

58. "The prophetic is selective. It responds to those who appreciate it and place value on it to pull for themselves that which the prophetic can do for them." - ADP

59. "You cannot use talk and conversations to win. You use instructions." - ADP

60. "Pilots do not fly by experience alone - they fly by instructions (a flight plan)." - ADP

61. "A pilot is trained to hear his name and know the number of his flight." - ADP

62. "Amidst the lots of talks he hears via the radio, he knows when his flight number is called." - ADP

63. "When God decides to raise a team of high flyers, He speaks the word to the church with all their weakness." - ADP

64. "But to Israel the man of strength and power, He brings His life-giving instruction." - ADP

65. "You do not fly by word alone. You fly by specific instructions." - ADP

66. "When you see a non-flyer in the body of Christ, then you know that they are either ignorant of, hardened towards, rebellious of, or despise instructions." - ADP

67. "When God decides to raise a team of high flyers, He uses instructions." - ADP

68. "Within those instructions lies shortcuts to any and every miracle you need in life." - ADP

69. "Whatever you desire to have today requires process, but within the process are shortcuts." - ADP

70. "The shortcuts are hidden and encapsulated in specific instructions." - ADP

71. "If your life is always going through long paths, I can tell that you are missing instructions." - ADP

72. "Whenever God gives you instructions, He is licensing you to take shortcuts to big things legally." - ADP

73. "For Moses, the instruction received did not divide the sea." -

ADP

74. "The instruction acted upon was what divided the sea." - ADP

75. "You like to fly, but you do not know what it is costing the pilot to hear the instruction." - ADP

76. "Show me a lover of instructions and one who adheres to destiny instructions, and I will show you a potential high-flyer in life." - ADP

77. "Becoming a high-flyer requires that you are addicted to receiving, processing, acquiring, and applying instructions to your life." - ADP

78. "It is too heavy to tell and translate to a man that when he acts in obedience, he can command the miracle he desires." - ADP

79. "The promised land is waiting for you." - ADP

80. "The land has milk and honey, but the shortcut of where you are going to requires specific instructions." - ADP

81. "God permits stubbornness because He is about to put His glory on display." - ADP

82. "Every time God gives specific instructions, miracles are released." - ADP

83. "When a prophet gives you shortcuts, it keeps you connected with the prophet for the rest of your life." - ADP

84. "God wants you to be so knowledgeable of kingdom things that men should come to you for guidance." - ADP

85. "You live life against the contradictions that eventually the world will learn how to live from you." - ADP

86. "Every human wants a shortcut to what they seek. The question is who is authorizing your path?" - ADP

87. "God desires to raise a set of people that will be high-flyers." - ADP

88. "People who will fly by instructions and become the envy of their generation." - ADP

89. "The strength of a pilot is not in the number of years he/she has had their license, but it is in the number of hours he/she has successfully flown or acquired." - ADP

90. "You have to pass the test of mercy and compassion to the undeserving so that God can use you any day and time." - ADP

91. "The secret - God cannot go anywhere alone. He is called the Lord of hosts." - ADP

92. "Any and every time God moves, He travels with all the angels." - ADP

93. "We fly by instruction." - ADP

94. "If you want to be a high-flyer, it is your responsibility to master the art of discerning specific instructions." - ADP

95. "There are certain destinies you can never fulfill until you master the art of listening to divine instructions." - ADP

96. "No alternative. Serve God and God alone." - ADP

97. "A lifetime of sweetness is your portion." - ADP

98. "God has an agenda. When He gives you instructions, and you follow, you will find yourself living a lifetime of solutions and possibilities." - ADP

99. "When you operate in the dimension of the Lord, difficult things begin to service your destiny." - ADP

CONCLUSION

ow that you are concluding this journey through wisdom's corridors let us address the most crucial element between knowledge and transformation: "Action." Although the Wisdom Capsules shared in this book hold tremendous power, I want you to know that they will remain merely theoretical until you take decisive steps to implement them in your daily life. Knowledge without application is like a seed never planted; it holds potential but produces no fruit.

The time has come to move beyond passive reading and contemplation into purposeful action. Each principle you have encountered in these pages beckons you to step out of your comfort zone and into practical application. Your destiny isn't waiting for more information; it's now waiting for your implementation. Don't forget that the most outstanding achievers in history weren't necessarily those who knew the most but those who acted decisively on what they learned. The wisdom you now possess is sufficient to begin your journey towards an extraordinary life.

Don't fall into the trap of eternal preparation, constantly seeking more knowledge while postponing action.

Start where you are!

Start with what you know!

The time for transformation is now. Not tomorrow, not next week, not when conditions seem perfect.

A SPECIAL CALL TO SALVATION & NEW BEGINNINGS FROM APOSTLE DR. DAVID PHILEMON

Dear Beloved,
God loves you deeply and has brought you to this moment for a reason. No matter your past, His love and forgiveness are available to you.

The Bible says in John 3:16, "For God so loved the world that He gave His one and only Son, that whoever believes in Him shall not perish but have eternal life." Jesus Christ came to save you, offering you a new life of purpose and peace.

If you're ready to accept Jesus as your Lord and Savior, pray this simple prayer:

The Salvation Prayer

"Heavenly Father, I come to You in the Name of Jesus. I acknowledge that I am a sinner in need of a Savior. I believe that Jesus Christ is Your Son, that He died for my sins, and that You raised Him from the dead. I repent of my sins and turn to You with my

Whole heart. Jesus, I ask You to come into my life. Be my Lord and my Savior. I surrender my life to You. Fill me with Your Holy Spirit, guide me on the path of righteousness, and help me to follow Your script for my life. Thank you, Father, for saving me. In the name of Jesus. Amen."

Welcome to the Family of God!

If you have just prayed this prayer, Congratulations! You are now a child of God, and heaven is rejoicing. Your journey has begun, and we're here to support you as you grow in faith and discover God's unique plans for you.

Next Steps:

• Connect with a Bible-believing church.

• Read the Bible Daily: God's Word is your guide.

• Pray Regularly: Prayer is your lifeline to God.

• Share Your Faith: Don't keep the good news to yourself.